SOMETHING
Unexpected

Jully

Order this book online at www.trafford.com
or email orders@trafford.com

Most Trafford titles are also available at major online book retailers.

Printed in the United States of America.

ISBN: 978-1-4269-6326-1 (sc)
ISBN: 978-1-4269-6327-8 (e)

Trafford rev. 04/04/2011

 www.trafford.com

North America & International
toll-free: 1 888 232 4444 (USA & Canada)
phone: 250 383 6864 ♦ fax: 812 355 4082

For my sister and all of my friends
I love you guys.

On October 25th of the year 2001 my favorite and most trusted friend past away, my father. He was very funny and friendly and filled with determination. Every time our 1967 Chevy Impala broke down, dad would always leave the hood for last. He would check everything first and wait until I got home from school to help check inside of the hood. Dad was one of those fathers who would never let the apprentice just hold the light, he'd had me multitasking. I always was happy at the end of it all, because dad's shimmery blue eyes would always look down on me as if he were to tell me that he was more than just proud of me, but that was years ago. What had once been a fantastic routine has become only but a humble memory in my mind.

I will never get to see his eyes spark anymore or even feel the oily grease upon his beautiful cheeks. I will never hear his sweet and smooth laughter or smell the scent of burnt rubber that came from his long and wavy dark hair. Unfortunately, I will never get to be a flying jet airplane in his soft and warm hands as he'd made it seem..., never again.

It's been nine years since my father's "tragic and extreme accidental car crash." I still go to his grave and tell him about the things I know he would want to know. Once a week after school I would go down there with lovely Irises for him. My father didn't exactly like flowers, but he was quite fond of the color. I only do go there once a week because The Store only sells Irises once week. I tell my father how much smarter Wesley has gotten since the last time dad has seen him, when Wes was too young to be able to remember dad. I talk to him about how badly things are going...with the Chevy Impala I'd begged mom not to throw away like some sort of worthless "trash bucket." Sometimes I would whisper to him the kind of home we live in. The kind of "guardian/s" we are forced to have ever since mom was declared insane and had gotten herself on house arrest a little while back.

http://www.google.com/imgres?imgurl=http://
www.chevroletimpalapic.com/chevroletimpala/car/
pictures/2010/08/67-impala.jpg&imgrefurl=http://
www.chevroletimpalapic.com/page/60&usg=___g2m1U_
ORSWYqvfmW50wBXv-YFeI=&h=600&w=900&sz=92&hl=en
&start=6&zoom=1&tbnid=Wyz6A81H0sy_pM:&tbnh=165&t
bnw=242&ei=FZVJTY3ZJ8aAlAfu45wR&prev=/images%3Fq%
3D1967%2Bchevy%2Bimpala%26um%3D1%26hl%3Den%26s
a%3DN%26rlz%3D1T4ADSA_enUS396US399%26biw%3D100
3%26bih%3D505%26tbs%3Disch:1&um=1&itbs=1&iact=hc&
vpx=151&vpy=227&dur=1047&hovh=183&hovw=275&tx=1
71&ty=95&oei=D5VJTaSODIG88gbqg4ytDg&esq=2&page=2&
ndsp=6&ved=1t:429,r:3,s:6

'Till this day I regret the death of my father, but it's not as if I could do anything about that now. Losing part of my genes, my dominant allele, my *inheritor* has made a big difference in our life. My father's absence has not changed my personality, but it has created a giant crater in my heart. In that huge, empty space, there used to be love. Now faster and faster the crater becomes filled with hate, despair, and cold blooded anger, but my face expression will never give that away. Well, maybe his absence has changed me. Maybe I used to be that little, humble, playful, and smiling girl before he did what he did. Now, I'm not little and humble and playful, and I'm not as smilingly as before because I grew up. It took me three weeks to grow up, become wiser, and become independent, though I had to be independent with Wesley by my side.

Wes needs me a little more than what I need him. He needs a firm hand over his shoulders, but he also needs a gentle one as well and I can manage both. Wes is a good kid with a simple rough start, but I will do all that I can to make sure Wes finishes smoothly. It is after all my job to look after Wesley, I know dad would be proud of what I had become...

for Wesley. I've become more than just the older sister, maybe now I'm his savior. I'd become the person Wes could count and counted on to save him, and so I can't have him doubt me...ever.

One cloudy, cold, and windy fall morning in our *lovely* home I woke up to the smell of eggs, bacon and...burnt toast. When I opened my bedroom door the smell slapped me like a pile of bricks. I could manage to slip downstairs quietly in my sexy hot pink and black pajamas with my piglet slippers. I was afraid to enter the kitchen and so I just stood behind that old wall, waiting for something unexpected. Sooner or later the sound of my rumbling gut gave me away. I soon heard footsteps becoming louder and louder, slowly. So I tried to make my way back up the stairs. I felt like a convict running away from the cops or something around those lines. I tried to be as quiet as possible but this house is pretty old and it's not as strong as before, back in the days.

"*Excuse* me." Mom said from behind me.

'Not fast enough', I thought. So, I turned to face her. Her eyes weren't black or bloodshot red, they were, dare I say it, normal. She also didn't smell like cigarettes, that's a first. Mom's hair was brushed back into a gentle and classy ponytail, her messed up bangs were to the sides of her face. I think she was wearing mascara and lipstick. I could also swear I smelled a gentle and light pinch of perfume coming from behind her apron. 'Something unexpected is highly true.'

"There is food down here in Planet Hungry if you are."

'She's trying to make a joke, really, what for?' I asked myself.

"I'm not hungry." I lied.
"Well, I think your stomach won't say the same." She looked down at my slippers and then back to my eyes. "Get dressed and come eat something." She said more firmly and less gently.

I shook my head to let her know I understood and she went back into the kitchen. I had no idea what just happened; my drunken mother became sober? 'Unrealistic.' I rushed myself to the room next to mine. Wesley was sleeping in his bed. The baby crib was left untouched, and the laundry basket, too. I walked next to where his head was at and I patted his shoulder. My deep-sleep brother wouldn't wake up after a minute of patting. 'When the only odd fails you get loud,' I usually tell Wes. I opened the window curtains, the sun came out from behind the dark clouds at times. It was so bright, compared to the darkness inside that I could have begun to growl with anger.

I then turned on the light in the room and turned off his fan decorated with Spider-man stickers. I also turned on his alarm, because Wes puts the alarm all set to go before going to sleep and turns it off when he gets up for a midnight snack. I then took the covers and blankets off of him and threw them on his sapphire color carpeted floor. The last thing I did was get on his bed. I started to jump up and down like the little innocent girl I used to be. 'Nothing.' Wesley was still sleeping. Then, after two or three minutes of jumping, the alarm rang. The sound came to me harder, faster, and more unwelcomed than the breakfast smell, I was almost thrown off the bed by the shock. As for Wes, the sound of a thousand trumpets and blow horns and whistles singing to Für Elise didn't "calm" him as much as it did me. Wesley crashed onto the floor. Alas, I could stop jumping.

"Are you crazy!? I was sleeping! It's Friday, plus no school! What part of no school did not go through your extremely *tiny* ears?" Wesley teased with a roar.

"Calm down, Bobo's sleeping. Mom's downstairs, though." I got off of the bed and watched as he turned belly-up on the floor.

"Yeah, like every morning!" Wes yelled; his mouth, eyes, and belly were the only thing that he would move.

You see, when Wes gets mad he stays still, trying to not be out of control or anything. I showed him this trick of mine the first time mom slapped him, when he was about five back then and yet he hasn't gotten any better at it.

"Are you ever going to shut your huge mouth anytime before the next ice age?" I leaned in over him, teasing him in my own big sister way.

He growled quietly and turned his face to face the bottom of his bed just like I knew he would.

"Mom cooked breakfast." I started slowly. "She bushed her hair. Make-up is on her face," I placed on accent on the word make-up, "Her eyes aren't black. She's wearing perfume, too." I had to sit down on his bed then.

"Stop making jokes. That'll never happen." He looked at me then.

I stood up and went to stand in the in-between of the door.

"I'm not the one making jokes today, Wes. Get dressed, we got plans." Then I left.

As I walked to my room I could hear him yelling, "What the hell does that mean?" Wesley has the attitude and the attention span of a ten year old.

After I had gotten fresh, dressed, and ready I waited for Wesley downstairs in the kitchen. Mom served me a plate of the breakfast she made even after I refused; I didn't want to eat anything she touched.

"You have to eat somethin'!" She barked out.

"No, I don't." I said calmly, slowly, and almost with an attitude.

Eye to eye contact with her is like feeding a pig bacon, it's just plain wrong. My eyes were either on the kitchen entrance or quietly examining the food.

"I'm not going to let you starve to dead, Owlina Misty Parker!"

'Oh, hell no!' She said it. 'No way! She's dead. She's freaking dead.' Bitch. 'No, forget it. Calm down and forget it.' Why? '1, 2, 3, 4, 5, 6, 7, 8, 9, 10. It's 1 and carry the 10 plus 7 over 9. 20 and 5. 1, 5, 8, 651, and 32.' I count to calm down as well. I then tried to change the subject in my mind. 'Now you care? Where was that sympathy I needed when your messed-up self wouldn't feed me for weeks and dad had to feed me behind your eyes? Where was that sympathy that I needed when I was three?'

"Maybe you should! Let me die, then you'll only have two tormentors in your life!" I stood from the chair.
"What are you talking 'bout?"
"Grandmother Sophie has a big mouth, you know."
"Just like you. Now sit down and eat!" I felt something that came from her. The precise word should be solicitousness.
"I have to go."
I walked to the door and got a grip on the handle, she followed behind me.

"You are... always going somewhere and leaving me alone. I need a life too, you know?"

'No.'

"You're job is to look after Bobo while I'm gone. He's your son; make a life out of being a good mother to him."

'Cause you sure as hell aren't a good one to us.'

"I am a good enough mother...to all of you! You just don't see it!"
"Of course you are." I said sarcastically.
"I feed you."
"When you fell like it, or when your freaky disorder mood swings become normal." I turned my head to see her red face, her red, angry, and irritating face.
"I comfort you!"

"The only time I could possibly recall that is in my dreams. Completely unreal and unproven to be an actual memory."

A tear fell from the corner of her left eye. She curled in her lips and nodded her head up and down. She then walked away to the dining room. Finally, Wes came down when I saw her laying down on the mahogany table.

"WHAT THE HELL ARE YOU DOING? That's not a fucking bed, dumbass!" I barked out.

She was still sleeping on the table after about a minute. She slipped down to the chair and glided her head down to the table.

"Ready?" I asked Wesley.

"Yeah."

Wesley wore his favorite T, his torn up jeans, and his favorite blue, black, and white Airwalks. He also brushed his pretty long, wavy, and light hazel hair down. It's now up to the bottom of his head, it looks good on him.

"What's that?" I looked down. He was carrying an old smelly shoe box. It really reeked.

"Franklin VI." He responded.

His goldfish. This one was special, because this one little and brave fish lasted an entire month. Franklin VI won a great war. To be honest Franklin VI is actually the first, but its Wesley's fish…, was.

"Let's get moving." I opened the door, when I turned back to face him he was looking at mom. She had fallen asleep on the table again. By now her bedroom must have spider webs by the dozen. Wesley's face couldn't have been more shocked. When we where just off of the porch our neighbors decided to drop in on us, like usual. Not unexpected.

"How's it going, guys?" Asked, a much energetic, Nick.

"Yeah, how's your day today, guys?" Asked a similar Beck.

"How are you two doing in this fine morning?" Lux asked.

The Tucker Triplets.

"We're good, what about you?" I asked a bit scared of what the answers might be.

"I'm okay. But a bit sad, 'cause I was playing on my bike with my cousin on his and when we were racing I fell and scrapped my knee. Then, I tried to get up and I couldn't and somehow I woke up the next morning with a cast over my leg. You see?" He pointed to his left leg. "Everyone signed it and brought me candy and bears and get-well cards and balloons, but I can't play on my bike anymore." Nick answered.

Ask Nick a question and you will receive a long and fast story. Amazing how fast they could speak, but then again they are highly, somewhat, developed nine-year-olds.

"I'm really good. Last night I played checkers and chess in the computer for 17 hours straight. I beat 62 kids in China, 12 in Japan, 19 in Hawaii, 7 in Colorado, 19 in Canada, 2 in Italy, and 17 in Melbourne. Then, I got grounded for not cleaning my room, but then I wasn't grounded because I cleaned my room and I was being good. In the morning, today, now, mom made my favorite breakfast and said that we are going to the Science Center today for my early birthday present. See, I'm here wearing this," He patted his oversized blue T., then his duck shorts, and pointed to his muddy shoes, "because dad said that I'm not allowed to get my new clothes dirty, so I'm changing later into my science lad coat and goggles when it's time to go." Beck answered.

Ask Beck a question and you get a long and slow and almost moving story.

"This fine morning fits my profile, I'm very content. I am already having a breathtaking day." Lux answered.

Ask Lux a question and you will receive...not much, with a pinch of something more.

"Cool?" Wesley *tried* to make it sound convincing.

"That's good. Well, we'll see you guys later." I said as we walked to the sidewalk.

"No, don't go. I wanna play." Nick said.

"No, the Science Center ain't until three hours away." Beck said.

"Bye, guys. I'm going to go inside and play hangman with Chris." Lux said.

Chris being their older brother.

"Sorry, Nick. So sorry, Beck. Bye, Lux. But we got plans, boys." I told them.

"Bye, guys." Wesley said.

They ended up letting us go and wrestling on their front yard. 'Boys.' It took us about five minutes to get to the stop, the bus stop. Then, another ten minutes to get to the graveyard.

"Hey, Justin." Wes said as we got closer and closer to the gate.

"Hey, buddy. What's that you got there?" Justin asked.

He put down the hose near an old and extremely and beautiful willow, my really nice willow, and ran to open the gate for us.

"Franklin VI; 'He was a brave warrior,' or that's what she said." Wes pointed to me.

"Well, why don't we go to The Store and see what we can do for this one." Justin scrambled Wesley's hair and then ran to finish watering the plants.

I closed the gate behind me and waved hi to him. He smiled his bright and gorgeous smile and that's it. I walked with Wes to The Store. At The Store you can get everything you need to burry someone, or even flowers, or grass, or even a personalized tombstone. I bought Wesley a gorgeous little red casket and he picked up the flowers and the shovel. I would return for the tombstone. The casket is small enough for me to carry, and small enough to fit a dead goldfish in. The sunflowers were Franklin VI's favorite, or so Wesley says. And so, after about twenty minutes of burring Franklin VI we returned to The Store. I bought two Irises. I only buy two Irises to represent dad's two children, Wesley and me. Bobo is our half-brother. According to "that lady" she's not sure who Bobo's real father is. She thinks the father is some guy she met at the liquor bar one night and ended up having an orgasm with him. The thought of Seashell sleeping with some drunken stranger is not entirely shocking. And yes, her name is   Seashell. I come from a whole line of drunken parents. But, what does she know? She forgets her own name at times.

Wesley and I each placed an Iris on the ground right besides the stone that read, "Ricky Lucifer Parker R.I.P. Dear and Beloved father, husband, son, uncle, brother, and cousin." I had them change it and put father first rather than husband.

"I love you, pops." I heard Wesley whispering a few times.

"I got a B plus on my Science quiz, dad. You knew it; you knew I would pass the semester, didn't you?" I told dad a bit louder than how Wesley was talking.

"Franklin VI died last night. He lasted through a whole month."

"He went through the toughest war of his life if he was your pet." I raddled Wesley's hair.

"So you say." Wesley quoted me with a smile, but knowing my brother he was becoming angry.

"Dad, mom looked different this morning. She had perfume and make-up. She brushed her hair and everything, pretty scary either way. Oh, and made breakfast, how weird is that, dad?" I asked.

After a few minutes Justin came from out of nowhere in the graveyard's ginormous lawnmower. 'Not unexpected.'

"Hey, you done, kid? Lend me a hand?" Justin asked loudly.

Wesley thumbsed-up "Jaystin." He then kissed the tombstone and said once more, "I love you, pop..., always." Then, he went to sit next to Justin on the lawnmower seat. We do this every week, to let me and dad have some time.

"See you later, okay?" Justin waved to me.

"Later." I waved back as I nodded my head; I probably looked silly.

"Bye, Owl." Wes said.

"*WESLEY!*" I barked out.

"... Oh, sorry. But..., you later, Al." Wesley sort of apologized.

"Yeah! You know what. Just get the hell *out* of here." I turned my back to them.

Call me Al or nothing at all. How could Wesley forget the most important rule?! How can he forget that he's not allowed to say that name?! 'This was something that I should've expected!' Damn it!

"...Al, I'm sure he didn't mean to." Justin said softly.

"Go, Justin." I said with a pitch in my voice. I always try to watch my tone with Justin; he deserves that at least that much from me.

I pointed somewhere, anywhere, as long as it was away from me.

'Forget it. Forget it. Forget it. Forget. Forget it. Forget it.'

After they left it was just me and dad. In some parts of the one-way conversation I felt like crying, but dad hates to see me cry, even if they're happy tears. An hour later I stood up and kissed the tombstone.

"Until next week, dad." I said with nothing more than dried eyes.

I walked slowly around the extremely ginormous cemetery. At first I was just looking around for Justin and Wesley, but then I figured that Wes was already in good hands. I know that for a fact. Justin goes to my school and he's a pretty good kid academically. But it was December 17th, 2008 that made me realize how good of a person this older guy really is.

I was having "one of those bad days" that day. I slipped on the ice below my feet as I was getting off the bus. I tried to stand up, but I couldn't get a grip from anywhere around me. If I cared two cents on how I look, I would have to say that I might have looked ridiculous. Not to Justin. I held on to his arm as if I have known that it was there all along. When I got on my feet he handed me my backpack and told me, "Don't even say it." He sounded serious. At breakfast the milk spilled all over my shirt. Justin was right next to me in the blink of a black eye-liner covered eye. He took off the shirt he had on and handed it to me. Abs as beautifully shaped as mountains or birds were right there in front of me. Gorgeous russet color skin covered them. They seemed as soft as an untouched swirled ice cream cone. As he took out an undershirt from his backpack he told me, "That's two plus a shirt." Walking up the stairs to 8th period I stepped on gum. But this gum was no ordinary gum, not according to my calculations. It was some sort of edible, mutated, strength gaining, unbreakable, kryptonic gum. My leather combat boot was as weak as fish number 1 was against Wesley. Then, out of the corner of my eye I see him again. "Give me another minute," he told me. He took off his boots and untied mine. I was soon free and in someone else's shoes, seriously. Justin took out a knife and cut my boot free. He handed me the pair after he tucked it back in, somewhere. "Don't tell?" He said. I replied as I looked down to my feet, "That's three plus a shirt and a pair of boots." He smiled and left me. At the end of the day I found him wearing some other pair of boots. Maybe he's psychic. It was some day, a bad day, almost.

I hid behind my number 1 tree. The other willow tree is just no comparison to this one, the mother of all mother-roots. This willow tree is the one I love. I actually told   everyone how badly I want to be buried under or at least right beside it when I die. This will happen or there'll be a few souls to haunt before I go into "the light."

But as I was finishing my admiration, I began to realize something. There was a girl leaning in front of a tombstone. Her curly, long and dark brown hair was falling down over her shoulders and elbows. She also had this gorgeous black beret, very nice. The girl also had a long dark gray coat; seemed soft. She looked quite nice and dressed in Paris clothing. I fell in love over her boots and her turquoise skinny jeans. Her boots made me think of the horrible kryptonic gum. But her skinnies were my favorite color, so it was normal for me to have-

"I can hear you, you know."

'How?'

She then stood up straight, but she didn't face me. She was pretty tall, about my height. At least I didn't get that from Seashell, she's a midget.

"Come here. It's not a private area if you want to come, you know."
And so I did. I tried hard not to trip over any twigs or logs on my way there. When I did walked around her and the tombstone, to face here since she wouldn't face me.

"Hi." She said kind of cheerfully, semi, and with a smile.
She blinked those gorgeous green eyes of hers three times, quickly, and she had me locked. She opened her mouth; rosy lips; and I wanted to know what she had to say. She moved her hand to move a piece of hair from her face and I was mesmerized.

"I'm Ariadne. Call me Aria if you like."
"Hi." I responded and she giggled once.
I looked down. She smiled at me, though, I couldn't see it I could feel it.

"My sister, Ananaisa. We called her Isamarie Bell..., because she liked it more. She had this depression thing that killed her. What about you? Who are you here for?" She seemed interested.
"My dad, Ricky. He got into this 'tragic and extreme accidental car crash.' I came every week ever since.
"Since?" She asked.
"2001. This place has been like home to us since."

"… That's a lot of time. I only come once a month, when my brother doesn't clean her tomb and stuff." Aria responded.

'Wesley.' I started to look around. No sign of Wesley or Justin or and a lawnmower insight.

"Sorry." She tried to grab my attention. I t worked. "I'm holding you up, sorry. Please go, I didn't mean to."

"… No, it's okay." I stopped my searching and looked at her. "The only duty I got is short and driving around in a ginormous lawnmower."

"Ah, I see. Uh…, brother?" She asked.

"Wesley." I answered quickly.

"Ginormous lawnmower? Is he with Justin?"

"You know Justin?"

"As well as I know my better half. Justin's my brother, older by 3 years and he won't let me forget it.

"I didn't know he had a sister…, sisters."

"No one ever does, he keeps to himself more than he really should."

"He speaks to me." I pointed out.

"…For some odd reason."

'For some odd reason?' I repeated this in my head. What does that mean? That he doesn't talk to people or… people like me? Me trying to answer my own questions never helped me before and it won't help now.

"But you are pretty, so it could be that. And you have nice hair… and really gorgeous eyes. Heck! If he doesn't fall for you I will." She joked.

I think she was joking. I only smiled with nothing more to say.

"But seriously, he talks to you? That's weird. Even for Justin. You know, he's not known as Mister Social around here."

"What do you mean?" I was actually paying attention.

"We moved to Phlox from Parkview. Justin...," She stopped to turn her back to me. She started walking slowly, as if we were walking together or something like that, "had a life back in Parkview. He had a really sweet job back there. He had his tournaments and his trophies, which never made it from the move. Justin had Penny." She turned to face me. This time she walked even slower coming back. And she moved her hands while she was talking; I guess it's to signify intensity. "He loved Penny and Penny really loved Justin. He was happy with her. They had plans together, after high school. She told me once that she was pregnant, but had an abortion with his kid. But mom wouldn't hear it. She only wanted to move so that they wouldn't be together. I still don't know why he likes you and your brother, if he is babysitting. He doesn't make sense." Then she stopped walking to stand exactly where she was at before.

"The Justin I know is always happy and making my day."

She gave me the "are you going crazy" look. The same one I got from Wesley this morning.

"What?" I asked with a "friendly attitude."

"... Come with me." She went around the tombstone and firmly grabbed my arm.

She was pulling me towards The Garage. The Garage is about sixty feet behind The Store.

"Why are you pulling me?"

'Pretty strong.'

"Cause I need you to hurry up and by what I've seen you aren't very fast."

'True, but so what.'

When we got there she released me very unhappily. I had a red mark on my left arm.

'The mark was something expected.'

"Justin Robert Van Berg!" Ariadne barked out.

"Shhh, I'm right here." His head popped out from behind two curtains framed on the border on the middle of the garage. "What?"

"Huh! Do you know this girl?" She started slowly.

"Yes. Yes, I do." He answered.

"... Do you *talk* to her?" She almost chocked when she was saying the word talk.

"Yes, Aria."

"..." Her hard expression began to turn into confusion rather than acceptance. "And are you two... like friends?"

"Yes, Ariadne!" Justin began to become irritated. "What is this, an intervention?"

"Calm down, Justin." I could barely hear her now. "I just didn't know. But now I'm concerned. Did you and your stupid self forgot all about Penny? Did you?"

"Ariadne!" Justin's whole body came from behind the curtains and walked closer to us. "I am not talking to you 'bout this! You should jus' mind your own business and get out of mine. Or at least find a life!"

"... Justin." She whispered.

"Get out of here." He said more softly.

I'm glad me and Wesley don't argue like this. This seems almost barbaric.

Aria turned her back to him, slowly, and as she walked to the door she said, "You can come with me if you want."

"I don't want to go anywhere with you." Justin answered.

She stopped right on the twilight zone of the door and faced us.

"And I wasn't talking to you, Dumbo." Her finger pointed to me.

"She has a name." Justin said.

"Well, I don't know it." She placed her hand down now.

"..." I gave Justin the worst look ever. The "I'm going to kill you" look. "Al." Justin said to Aria.

'Thank goodness!'

"Well, you can stay here or come with me, Al." She told me.

I looked down to my still in pain arm and said, "Thanks, but no thanks."

"What's that?" Justin was talking about my new mark. He looked over my hand that's was trying to cover the mark, not very well, though. "Ariadne!"

"... Let it go, Justin." I whisper so low that I could bare catch that.

"Thanks, but no thanks." He teased. "Ariadne, go home."

"Al, are you sure?" She asked me once more.

"Yes." I answered quickly.

"... Alright, maybe next time I'll get to meet your brother." She said.

'Not by the hair of my chiny-chin-chin.'

"Go!" Justin urged.

Ariadne eventually left and Justin had to calm down sooner or later. He brought me a small, cold and wet towel to put over my arm. He takes good care of me.

'For some odd reason.'

We sat on old boxes, talking. Wesley came out from behind the curtains after a few minutes. He was smiling as he found a box for himself. Both were smiling.

'What's through those curtains?'

"Yeah, Aria does have her moments, though. I bet it's hard to believe that now. Look, I'm sorry again about that."

"Justin! Please, do me a solid favor and STOP apologizing." I said.

"... I don't think I can, sorry."

"Ha-ha." Wesley laughed.

'At least someone's enjoying himself.'

After a few more minutes of hearing Justin apologizing and I was done. I told him that I would see him later and Wesley fist punched his fist and said, "Later, yo."

"Come by tomorrow, Al. I got something for you." Justin said when Wesley was handing him the towel I was holding.

"Justin." Wesley rushed in a whisper mixed with curiosity.

"Slow your horses, buddy. You're clean." Justin said and winked to him.

A sign of relief came from Wesley. Even stranger, they have secrets, together. Well, cant do anything about that, might as well just let it go.

"Tomorrow?" I asked.

"Yes." He said in a smart tone. "Come by anytime, I'll be here all day, but you must come by." He was folding the towel.

"Can I come?" Wesley asked.

"Well, it wouldn't be a party without you. But I doubt that Al would leave the house without you, so..., yes."

"I hate parties, Justin." I pointed out.

"I do, too." He threw the towel into a bucket about ten feet to his right. "That don't mean that I'm going to give you a party, no matter how much you want one." Teasing again.

"Well, alright, tomorrow. Here?" I asked.

"Whatever! Just be here!" He laughed.

I smiled at him as he was still laughing when we got to the door. Wesley winked at Justin and Justin nodded. Oh, the secrets. I looked down at my arm to see how good of a doctor Justin is and by the results he is a darn good one. My arm had absolutely nothing there, nothing. It only itched now and as I was scratching it he stopped me.

"Water, ma'am. Cold and preferably Vaseline under that. You hear?"

"Yes, Dr. Van Berg. I hear you loud and crystal clear."

We left Justin to finish his duties. I bought milk and cookies and a new lamp at a store about two blocks from the cemetery. Heading home to mom and Bobo is important.

"Mom! Mom!" I yelled as I entered the house.

The lamp went on an oak table that Aunt Karen gave mom for her birthday. The milk went in the fridge and the cookies in a plastic container, still no mom. I went upstairs to Wesley's room. Bobo was still sleeping in his little crib. I went to go pick him up and bathe him, but it seems like mom already did.

"I'm getting cookies, Al!" Wesley announced from the bottom of the stairs.

I walked out of the room and told him that I wouldn't dare him to. He wouldn't listen; I knew that much. So I just went back inside and took Bobo in my arms. He is a precious angel, a miracle and the other half of my life, though, Wesley covers most of it. Bobo is only about a year and a few months old. His little curls are almost up to light blue eyes. Wes and I have dark mixed with light green eyes. My hair isn't as light as Wesley's and Bobo's hair. Bobo will probably end up being a blonde, I CAN'T stand blondes. Though, Avril Lavigne gets away with it. Wesley has more of a light hazel color while I am more of a light brown, but it doesn't seem light in the dark. Anyways, Wesley and I don't look all that the same from Bobo. This strange and drunken man must have really been gorgeous if Bobo is as adorable now as he probably will be in the future.

"What?" A messed up haired, beer in her hand, trashed up, mom came through the door.

"Did you bathe Bobo?" I asked.

"*Yes*, *you* kinda told me to." She responded with an attitude.

"Well, don't do it again! I told you to be a good mother to him. I don't trust you with Bobo to give him a simple bath." My tone began to become softer. "Next time just feed him or something. And watch the temperature, and don't over feed him, he gets gassy and a stomach ache."

"Whatever." She rolled her eyes at me.

"Hey!" I yelled before she had a chance to go away. "This is your son. The one whose dad you don't remember.

The kid you *choose* to have no matter the consequences! I'm the one that has to be responsible for all of you, believe me or not. You know what? Just forget it. Don't even talk to him! If you could possibly... one day... have the potential to just feed him, then you may talk to him, but for now just stay away from   him. If he needs   you to do something and I'm not here, just do it. We'll see if your motherly instincts come to play one day."

She took a sip out of her bottle and shrugged her shoulders. She left soon after that without a word. Being responsible is a tough job, especially when you know you weren't exactly meant to be the responsible one for about three souls.

"Oh, sweet baby. Little angel, you don't deserve this, you or Wesley. You watch, one day, when I'm rich, I'll take you guys away from here. I'll take that old witch hag to the funeral home when she electrocutes herself. We all will have so much fun in the *Wichita Mountains. Wesley will take you on his mountain bike on an awesome ride, while I stay home cooking and cleaning and singing along to the songs on the radio while the sun shines down on our lovely home. The Latency, The All American Rejects most definitely, Orianthi, Nickelback, Linkin Park, Paramore, 30 Seconds to Mars, Shinedown, Green Day, Parachute and so many more are going to be playing on the radio, you'll love it. I'll love it. Wesley will love it. You'll have a blast. Unless, you grow up and decide that you want to go looking for your biological father, I wouldn't blame you. But whatever you decide to do, don't forget that I'm your sister, yours and Wesley's."* I kissed the gorgeous top of his head and took him with me downstairs.

Wesley was on the computer eating cookies and playing some Call of Duty game or something called like that. Mom was out on the porch, still drinking. John had come home. John DeVersio is her boyfriend. They've been together for about four weeks, he's sure he's not Bobo's dad. I believe him because he looks nothing like Bobo. He took a blood test and they aren't related in anyway. He was sitting on the porch with Seashell, he was smoking.

"You eating anything else?" I asked Wes.

"... GO! Go! Go now!" Wes yelled. "What the hell are you doing, Go!"

"Wesley." I said

"I'm eating, Al. Yo, go! Save yourself, will yah!"

"I'm making you some soup or something." I then left my idiotic brother to his life in the computer world of 1s and 0s.

"Thank you." I heard him exhale. "Farwell, my dear comrades."

I put Bobo in his highchair and went to go get the things for the soup. I could see Seashell and John on the porch from one of the windows in the kitchen. The water was in the pot and was not hot enough yet.

"And?" Seashell asked.

"You got to go. You know Al will want that…, Wesley wouldn't care…, and Bobo will thank you." John replied.

"You want me to go?" She asked.

"… I want you to feel better. This is going to make you feel better, so yeah. I want you to go." John said without a smile.

"What about the kids?" She asked.

"What about them? Al will take care of them. I can't take care of them while you're not here. I'll be over my sister's." He said.

"Well, I can't go anyways." She began to take quick shots out of the bottle.

'She will run out sooner or later.'

"Why?" He asked her.

She didn't answer; she was too busy enjoying her bottle of Heineken.

"Why?" He repeated the question to her again and got the same result.

After a few minutes of only getting to hear her swallowing John had stood up. He had a really irritated look upon his face. To Seashell it probably only looked like that because he must have ran out of cigarettes.

"Would you *please* take this seriously?" He begged her as he threw is lighten cigarette under his foot. He stumped on it and looked at her bottle. "Would you?"

The look on Seashell's face looked to be more timid than ever before, but yet she wouldn't stop taking shots.

"I'll be here right next to you. We'll get through this... together." John said as he went to go and sit next to her. Then, he took her left hand in both of his.

She stopped taking the shots to look at him. He was... crying.

'SHOOT.'

The water that was boiling was too much; it was spilling out of the pot. I turned it down and brought the things over to put into the pot. Wesley came into the kitchen to look at the catastrophe. He was laughing as I was in pain trying to get everything together. Bobo was apparently up and Wesley was feeding him part of his cookie.

"It looks like you could use a hand." Wesley pointed out.

"Can you feed him, please?" I asked as I was adding a pinch of chopped onions to it.

"… Hmmm…, I don't know." He was teasing.

"Please, Wesley. I'm not Wonder Woman." A carrot.

"Alright, but you owe me one." He smiled at Bobo.

"Really? Whatever, his food's in the fridge. Get him the apple sauce."

"Ma'am, yes, ma'am."

I owe him one? One what? What is it that he wants so much that he would have me begging for his help? This kid just gets weirdo and stranger by the hour.

After feeding Bobo Wesley walked over to the kitchen table and waited there, quietly and patiently. What would he know about being patient?

When I got over to him I asked him what was going on and he simply said, "Can you please serve me a bowl of soup?" The look on my face could not possibly describe to you the kind of sensation, confusion, which I had. But, I didn't question him, I just served him and that's it. I cleaned the dishes and cleaned the kitchen when everyone had finished eating. John and Seashell sometimes eat on the porch, I never complain about it unless they leave the dishes outside. But this time they ate outside and didn't forget anything. So far so good. Afterwards, I played a little bit in the living room with Bobo while John and Seashell were still outside and Wesley went out to play with the Tuckers. On TV I saw this really old lady on the news; she had gotten beaten by a bunch of younger kids, about my age or so. She was talking about how she's sorry that it happened; because it hurt, but how she wouldn't ever hold it against them, against anyone. She looked old enough to be 50 but she was 65, her light blue eyes were just adorable, her thin and long white as snow hair was gorgeous. I looked at her limbs and I thought that she was so skinny, but it was not because she didn't eat or because she was old, but because the bruises on her body were severe and some parts of her wouldn't work again. So, I guess she just decided to throw those parts out. Those parts that supported her throughout her life are now somewhere probably rotting.

"Whatever. You say yes and I say no. We're done." Seashell said as she came through the door.

"We aren't done, Sea! You got to and you're *going* to talk about this. I don't care if it's with me or not, just do." John replied. He, too, came through the door shortly after her.

"Go suck one, John!" She said from the fridge.

"Seashell! You know what, just shut up! Just shut the hell up, alright? And I'm *not* asking." John said. He was making his way up the stairs then.

"Be patient with her, John." I whispered to him before he had the chance to fully go up the stairs. I never took my eyes off of Bobo.

I heard his footsteps making their way down.

"*This* coming from *you*?" He asked from the stairs.

"Yes! And I just want to help, but since no one ever asks Al for shit anymore, forgive me."

"...I want to help too, but she just won't budge. Nothing we can do if she's like this. I'm done right now." He left up the stairs and that was it.

What's up with everyone lately? No one's acting like their self. It's like we just went from "normal" to being in a movie slash soap opera.

"*What* the hell is this?" She yelled.

I looked and she was standing next to the lamp I had just finished buying a little while ago.

"It's a lamp. You use it to make things brighter." I said as I looked at her funny.

'Dumbasses.'

"Smart-shit, that's not what I meant! What's it doing here?"

"Replacing the good one you broke." I gently tossed the small beach ball to Bobo.

"If there's a reason why I broke the other one then there's one for me waning to break this one." I looked at her right then.

"*Don't*. You. Dare." I growled.

She moved her left arm and it hit the lamp. I hassled to catch it. Time seemed to be going on forever; it was too slow for reality, or so it seemed. My arms stretched out as I dived under it. I felt like my efforts would be in vain. A minute later I had hit the carpeted ground. She was growling above me.

I caught it.

"..." I tried to find my voice under all of the anger. "Okay..., tell me...NOW, why you would do such a thing." I stood up and grabbed the lamp tight in my arms.

"I don't want a lamp here!" She roared.

"...Go upstairs." I pointed to the stairs.

I'm done with her medical drama. I guess that whatever's happening is happening to me, too. I hate to relate myself to any of them, expect the boys.

"Don't put a lamp there!" She demanded.

"Shut up and go upstairs."

She eventually did go upstairs with about three bottles of beer. She won't get it her way. I like this lamp and I want it here. So, that's where I put it.

Bobo was now still and quiet as we were watching Rugrats together, seeing him so focus is adorable. Well, I guess

I'm just a sucker for Bobo. A little while later and Wesley came in, he looked just about terrible.

"Wes?" I asked.
"...What?" He asked as he came into the living room.
"What happened?" I tried not to laugh.
"Aria's outside, looking for you!" He said, irked.

He ran his fingers through his now messed up beautiful hair and exhaled heavily. When he went upstairs to the bathroom I took Bobo and took a peek out of the window and into the front yard. Apparently, she was outside on the walkway in front of the door, she was very still. She just stood there, looking at the closed door in front of her. And so I went to the closet and took out one of Bobo's little jackets and put it on him. Then, I went to the door and opened it. She walked up to the porch and smiled at me.

"Hi Al, how are you doing?" She asked.

'Is she trying to make small talk?'

"Since a few hours ago, okay I guess." I answered.
"Good, good. That's good. And who's this?" She reached in to touch Bobo's face and I leaned him away.
"He's my other brother."
"...Listen, Al. I'm sorry about today. I really didn't mean to have hurt you like that. I didn't realize how bad it was until a while ago when Justin came home and told me about it. But it looks like you're all better."
"Justin takes good care of me and that's a proven fact." I said softly.
"He's a good guy. And also I'm here to apologize for dumping on you and Justin for being friends. It was just a shock to me. I mean he was going to be a father if Penny didn't had

thought about the abortion over and over again. I just can't help but think that you're his new Penelope. I'm sorry again."

Penny and Justin seemed to have had something pretty serious and strong. I have never thought of Justin that way, until now, so if one day Justin wants me and if I want him...I'll be ready for him. I know he'll take care of me. And when that day comes he'll forget about Penny.

"It's alright, Ariadne. I learned from an old lady not to hold grudges. You're clean." I quoted Justin.

"Well, thanks. And if Justin asks I wasn't here today. I'm supposed to be grounded and he would *freak* if he found out."

"Don't worry." I wouldn't hold it against her.

"I can't believe you're being this understanding. What's the catch?"

"Nothing, Ariadne. I won't say anything about you being here, you don't need to do anything for me, don't even clean my underwear. Just like that."

"It still makes no sense to me. I'm really, *really*, sorry about it all. Today I guess just wasn't my day for being nice. On my way here I ran over some little kid on Justin's bike. But I'll make this up to you, Al. Don't worry, I won't be left unpunished. I'll make sure of it."

"That sounds dangerous. Stay away from Ariadne, Ariadne."

"Ha-ha. Thanks...for giving me another chance. You won't regret it."

"All right." I said.

"...Before I go...," She started slowly, "Can I meet your little brother?"

Is she serious? She wants to meet Wesley? No, no, NO, NEVER!

"Maybe some other time." I told her.

A quick exhale came from her.

"All right, well then I guess I'll see you around."

"Yeah..., sure."

"Bye, baby." She whispered to Bobo.

So adorable, how Bobo waved goodbye to her as she kept saying bye to him. He just gets cuter and cuter. I saw as Ariadne stepping over a bike and picking it up. She left soon after that, I opened the door and looked inside of it. I saw stairs and that *hideous* carpet and Wesley coming downstairs, he still seemed mad. I took the liberty to just stay outside, stay out of all the madness for a second and enjoy the cool wind blowing by and the seeing the leaves fall down extremely slowly and to just spend some time for myself. I slipped Bobo through the door and let him crawl his way to Wesley in the living room. I then went to go sit on the top of the porch with my feet two stairs down. Everything made sense now, everything was peaceful now. I don't even have a jacket on and I feel just about as close to perfect as I can get. It's amazing its fall and it's amazing how happy I fell here, now, and I can feel that everything is just perfect and perfect is how I want it to stay, stay in fall in the perfect moment.

I wasn't counting minutes or anything, but I would assume that it was about ten minutes until I saw a bottle jet past the top of the roof above my head.

'Great, mom.' I just can't understand why that woman can't just stay still, shut up, and not do anything. Well, there goes my peace. 'I'll miss it.'

I walked in to the house and passed the kitchen, John had his face stuck in the fridge. I think he was looking for the ham that Seashell left in one of the upper cabinets. Then I got to the living room and Wesley was still upset, lying down on the couch with crossed arms. I don't like to see my little brother upset, he doesn't look nice with frown lines and well,

I just hate to have him upset in general. So I went by him and lifted his legs so that I could see next to him. His legs laid on my lap and I looked at him, I knew he knew that I was looking at him even if he was looking at the TV instead.

"Talk to me. What happened out there?" I asked, what I call, tenderly.

"... No." He never glanced at me.

"Tell me or I will tickle you Wesley Lucifer Parker." I was being serious.

"Don't." He looked at me then. "You. Dare."

"You *know* I will. So you *better* talk."

"Nick and Beck *tackled* me. How could I possibly compete with two people at once? Bustards."

"Oh, I see." I told him softly.

I looked at the TV; Wesley was looking at it, too. Bobo was falling asleep on the floor; I could see how badly he wanted to stay up to see how Tom tried to get Jerry this time. Sooner or later Bobo did fell asleep and I took him upstairs. He is so still when he sleeps, unlike Wes. He moves and moves and doesn't stop until he's knocked out in his sleep. When Wes was a baby I took him to bed, too, and it was fun, with Bobo it's more adorable than entertaining. I tucked him in with his favorite blanket. A red raspberry knit blanket that dad knitted when he was "into it." It was laying around for months under Wesley's bed until he had decided to give it to Bobo when he arrived. I don't think that Wesley completely understands what it means to be big brother. I think that he only knows how to be...my little brother. Only because Wesley was here first doesn't mean that my love differs for any of them, but Wesley is more fun, in his own way. Bobo   might   one   day get on my nerve for being so cute that I might stop loving him, at least that's my theory. So I'm enjoying him for if I do decide to do that to Bobo I would have had my time with him. When I went downstairs Wesley was sitting up and looking at me.

He blanks out sometimes and looks at people. I wonder if he really didn't mean to be looking at me or was he just being quiet and still here.

"Wesley." I said as I got closer to him.

"..." No respond.

"Wes, talk. What's going on?" I asked as I said next to him.

He was looking in front of him, where nothing stood, and yet where I was standing at.

"Wes, come on." I put my arm around him and he looked at me.

"Al," he began.

"Yes?"

"I want a tattoo."

"...Wes..., Wes..., Wesley, Please!" I stood up in shock and disbelief.

"Hear me out, Al. I'll look tougher; make it seem like if I didn't get tackled by two little kids."

'Oh, brother. Oh, *my* brother.'

"...Wesley, I doubt that anyone will think anything of it. No one will know." I kissed him forehead and kneeled in front of him. "I'll talk to the Tuckers. No worries, bro."

"No, Al. This is *my* fault." He looked down.

I laughed a little, quietly.

"And you're *my* brother." I said proudly.

"...Al, don't. They'll think I'm I wimp."

"This won't end well unless you let me help you, West star. I'll talk to Chris then. He knows he's little triplets and he'll put them to straight forms, considering that he *was* in the army for some time."

"...Al, you don't'-"
"Sugar biscuits!"
"...What?" He looked at me.
"Pop snaps!"
"...I love you, too." He said.

In the morning I heard the door knocking downstairs; no one ever gets the door in this house hole. I got out of bed and put on one of my little pajama pants that was laying around and slipped my piglet slippers on. I took out a jacket from the closet, I couldn't care more which one it was, and struggled to get my butt downstairs to the door. I opened it slowly and looked out. Jaystin. 'Completely unexpected.'

"Ha-ha." Justin tried to stop the giggles.
"... Hum, hey." I said. What more could I've said? Justin was standing on my porch, looking at me half naked and he's laughing.
"Nice slippers." Same old teasing Jaystin.
"...I'm sorry?" I don't' know, it slipped out.
"... Hum..., how are you, Al?" He asked in a rush.
"...Come in." I said as I opened the door wider.
He walked in gently into the little room in front of the stairs, right behind the door, and I closed the door. Winter's coming. The foyer was carrying a few leaves now.

"Wanna sit down?" I asked. "Thirsty, hungry?"
"... Uh?" He asked.
"Sit down, please." I pointed to the living room.
Once he'd finished taking his sweet time getting onto the couch I sat next to him and we talked.

"So..." I started.
"I know she came yesterday. She told me. I'm still sorry." He pointed out.

"Jaystin." I looked down.

"I am."

After a few minutes of silence he talked.

"Where's Wes?"

"Ha-ha. Sleeping, that kid doesn't wake up that easily."

"Well, you know how I told you to come by today?"

"...Yes." I answered softly.

He put his left hand over my right one and told me, "Come outside."

Right then Wesley charged down the stairs like some crazed bull.

"You're here!" He said in a breath from the door frame.

Justin took his hand off of mine as quick as he could without Wesley noticing, but Wes had a curious look on his face when Justin did that.

"Let's go show her." Justin said.

"...But it's... Today isn't..." What's happening?

"It's okay. You got it?" Justin asked Wes.

Wesley nodded his head and pointed one finger out. Then, he ran upstairs.

"...Jaystin." My curious self said.

"Hold up." He looked at me with a smiled.

"Got it!" Wesley repeated as he came storming down.

Then Wesley stood in front of us with his hands behind his back. Justin stood up and walked next to him. I stood up, too.

"For your birthday we were waiting... " Wesley said.

"Until then I couldn't take it... " Jaystin said.

"We got you a present... " Wes said.

"Two to be exact... " Jaystin said.

"Here's to you... " Wesley said.

"Our special girl, Al." Jaystin finished.

Justin smiled down at Wesley and nodded to him. Wesley came closer to me and handed me something. It was rectangular and plastic...and it had a picture of me.

"MY LISENCE!" I yelled as I jumped in shock and then went back onto the couch to start jumping up and down on it.

Normally, I would only yell like that in my dreams, but this had to be an exception. It was my license! My driver's license! The thing I've been waiting for ever since dad died. It my guarantee that I could keep the Impala! I'm completely happy right now!

...Maybe that little girl hasn't completely left the building either.

I stopped running to go and wrap my arms around Wesley's shoulders and I started kissing his adorable cheeks like crazy. Then, I went and jumped on Justin. My arms were around his neck and his arms were around my waist, trying to keep me from falling.

"Thank you. Thank you. Thank you. Thank you." I whispered into his ear.

Afterwards, he slowly dropped me and I was standing in front of them with *my* license tightly gripped to my fingers like some crazy person would.

"One more, Al." Wes told me when my nerves were settling down.

"*What*?" I couldn't believe it.

"It's outside." Justin said.

For a second I was pretty speechless, but then I figured that it couldn't have been better than this so my hopes weren't that high.

I nodded to them and they each took one of my arms and walked me outside. It is freezing cold and I'm still half naked, so this better be worth it. They dragged me to the driveway, where dad's Impala stood tall and proud. Last time I saw it, a few months ago; it was still as wretched as it was the day it got into the accident. It's glorious, I don't know much about cars, even if I should by now, but this baby could shine. It shines and it glows. If only I hadn't quoted that.

I was speechless. I just stood there like a mindless zombie with her dreams in front of her and in her hand. The guys just looked at me..., me crying. I couldn't hold the tears. How can I? I then felt Wesley's hand wiping away the tears. 'So cute.' I looked down at him and kissed his forehead. A few deep breaths calmed me enough from my excitements. This was completely, one hundred perfect, worth it..., worth it all.

"...I..." In between my words I took more breaths. It was a lot to take in in just one second of looking at it. "... HA...! You-..." The tears came all over the place then.

"It's okay." Justin said as he took me in into his nice and warm coat. "Let's try it out." He said as he tried to warm me up.

"Yeah, it's freezing!" Wesley pointed out.

So, yeah. Wesley took the keys from out of his jacket's pocket and handed it to me proudly. I took to that car not fast enough. I opened it and unlocked the doors, the guys and I got inside of him in a heartbeat. I started the car way too slow... and I meant   to. I was *savoring* the moment, trying not to forget the first time I started this car without dad right by my side, but with my brother and friend by my side. Wouldn't you want to remember it if you were me?

I started the car and it purred back at me with nothing *but* love. I sensed he remember me...from a long time ago, like seeing an old friend at the super market for the first time in forever and a day. Or like hearing that one song you adored but sooner or later forgot of and like by a miracle it came back to you. This is how it felt... it felt like victory to me.

"Want to go for a ride, Al?" Justin asked from the backseat.

You might think I would, heck, I would think I would..., but no. I don't.

"...No, I'm good." I smiled at him from that little mirror on the windshield.

"...Really?" Wes asked.

"Really. I just wanna stay. Stay here." I leaned back in *my* car seat and closed my eyes.

'My car. My car. My car.' I repeated sadly in my mind. 'He used to be dad's car.'

Then, like magic Wesley said..., "Dad handed it down to you, Al."

'...He did.'

Then I went and lower the heater and turned on the radio. Yes. Yes. Avril Lavigne was singing Hot. I knew that *I* would be hearing this song somewhere *we* liked and *we* would be *enjoying* ourselves. Though, I didn't know that Justin was going to be with us...and Bobo wasn't.

"You like it?" I asked Wesley.

"YEAH!" He said as he was doing his air guitar in the seat next to me.

"...Ha-ha. Knew it." I whispered. "What about you?" I turned around to ask Justin.

"...Uh hum." He was having fun, I could see it.

I was in peace...for *two* days in a row. I couldn't have done it alone.

"...For two weeks, you name where, when, and for how long, you got it." I told them.

It took them a minute to get it. Wesley was all for it, he was agreeing his little heart out. Justin wasn't having it so much. He was looking out the window after he said no thanks. I had a confused looked on my face. I know! The *EXACT* same looked Ariadne got when she realized we were friends, that's the face I had.

"Why not, Justin?" I asked.

He looked at me and he couldn't say anything to my disappointed and shocked face, so he looked away to answer me and I leaned back to wait...and listen.

"...I don't need to have you as my personal slave for two weeks with nothing in it for you. Actually, forget the 'nothing in it for you' part, because even if there was anything in it for you I wouldn't want to have to take advantage of you."

"Sweet, but it's not taking advantage of me if I'm offering." I said softly.

From a sentence to the next, when did our conversation begin to sound sexual?

"...No, Al." He leaned in closer to me, "I'm okay." And he leaned back.

"Well..., my offer will still stand."

"When can we go eat ice cream?" Wesley asked when the song was over.

"...When I'm up; I'm still tired...and naked." I said.

"Sorry." Justin said; same old Jaystin.

"You're coming, too." I told him.

"..." Wesley was nodded to him uncontrollably. "... Guess I am."

"Yes!" Wesley yelled.

The next song eventually came on after a few words from some sponsors. Wesley knows most of the songs on this station, so he probably won't want me taking it off anytime soon. We all just sat there, in *my* car, listening to music. Listening to the music I *knew* Wes would like. I should go inside and bring Bobo down here to join the party. Though, like I said, Bobo might end up wanting to go and search for his real father one day and when that day comes I have to let him go and I will. I will also have to not include him with the plans I have planned out, and I should bring in Justin instead. Justin does seem to be around more that Bobo is ever. But I guess that I can't do anything until I officially graduate and go move to the *Wichita Mountains and   until Bobo grows up and finds out what he wants to do. Though, I love him I won't go with him in search of some man that left him, and Wesley won't go with him.*

After a while Wesley went inside and he said he was going to get ready for ice-cream later. I decided to go and drive Justin home. This was a once in a lifetime opportunity, I've never seen Justin's home, not even in pictures and he doesn't talk about his life at home, so all I know is that he has two sisters. Even though I know almost nothing about his life at home, I don't really need to. All I need to know is who Justin is. His life at home could mean less to me if he did make it seem like a big deal. But even if I'll like to know more, I won't ask him, and I won't need to, because it doesn't bother me all that much. Wes and Justin are like best friends so he probably knows some things. Wesley isn't the type of kid to just keep highly important questions, for him, to himself.

I took my time as I drove him home. Justin was in the passenger seat looking out of his window for most of the ride. When he wasn't he would be singing along to the songs on the radio or asking me questions about what I like. I would ask the same questions back, just so I wouldn't seem rude. He seemed to be quieter in the car than he did anywhere else. It reminded me of that day, that horrible and somewhat good day in 2008. Back when he would only talk a sentence with me and then walk away, that mystery was intriguing to me. I have to admit that he seemed...different. Like if in some other dimension I liked the mysterious side of him more than I do this one. At least then I didn't even know his name. Now all I have to look forward to is listing to him talk about him life at home...and Penny. Though, I highly doubt that he would ever talk to me about Penny...or that...that... I don't think I could say it.

Baby.

"Almost there." He told me as he looked out through the windshield.

We were on this extremely long road. The houses had trees but not big enough for them to hover over the road. I always wanted to walk under a place like that, somewhere were all I could notice are the trees and their leaves making out above me. That got me thinking. What if I was an ant? I *despise* ants, by the way. Like I've told Wes, I would become an exterminator just to go and have the prestigious pleasure of killing ants. Anyways, if I was the *size* of an ant and the trees were willows, the experience would probably be more than just simply amazing. Wouldn't it? It had to be.

"Turn here."

A narrow street was expecting me at the right turn. It was nice. It had an old wooden fence to one side, white. There were trees, orange and yellow. I don't like the color orange. I say that I could only like the color orange in the fall, my favorite season, because it looks nice this time of the year. But I find it changeling liking such a color. My ex-best friend's soft and glorious hair was orange. Maybe that's why.

About a few minutes later and it was the end of that road. Justin told me to take a left. It had seemed as those that narrow street was cut out from an entirely different magazine and pasted back there. This road was just...normal, traditional, American, and...boring. Back there, it had life... I don't like the sense that I got of being locked here. The kind of sense that wouldn't allow me to listen to the kind of music I listen to, or to dress in the kind of clothes I dress in.

"It's that burgundy one on the left." He said...almost 'sadly' like.

As I pulled up onto his driveway he looked for his backpack. I think it was on the backseat. Didn't he take it when he was moving to the front? He eventually found it and thanked me.

"Should I just come by when we're ready?" I asked before he could close the door.

"...Sure. Beep a few times, I'll come down." He said.

"Okay, so later, after I sleep."

"..." He smiled and lowered his head. "Sorry, I couldn't help myself. It was staring at me in the face in The Garage. It was time."

I thanked *him* and he lifted his head. Afterwards I watched him as he knocked on the door a few times. It looks like he was in a rush to get inside when someone opened it. Or was trying to have that person not look at me? Either way, whoever it was took a peak of me, and I did, too. She had short black hair, really straight. Her skin was pale and she looked a little familiar. Not enough to make me have déjà vu, but enough to make me realize that I might have seen her somewhere. Like when you see a movie and you really like one character. Months later you see that person again and eventually start to learn their name and sooner or later you become a fan. I probably have seen her, once or twice before.

After that I tried to get home, I'm pretty good with directions so I didn't really get lost. I got home and hurried to park the car, shut it off, lock it, and run inside. It was still as cool as before and I was as still tired as before.

I woke up around twelve or something around then and found Wesley and Bobo playing with the beach ball in the living room. I got ready as soon as possible, without trying to be in a rush, I was going to *drive*. It didn't feel real at first, I looked at my keys   in the chain on top of my dresser. It seemed as though it mucked me, it was challenging me to take it out, realizing that it was real this time and not just something else now. I remember taking the test months ago, because Wesley needed a ride back and forward from his practices and mom was always too drunk to drive, that and she couldn't ever find the dang it car keys to her truck that Aunt Karen gave her once. After a while later I just grabbed the keys and headed out of my door. I told Wes it was time to go and told John, who was feeding Bobo on the couch.

We went to the car and I opened it up. After I turned it on, Wes turned up the heater...and the volume. Tonight, I love you, The Latency. I pulled out of the driveway, driving has its perks. I liked it, so far. I looked at Wesley next to me and waited until he buckled up. When he did I started driving. The way to Justin's place didn't seem like it was that far, even though it is forever and a day away.

"Having fun?" Wes asked after a few minutes when the song was over.

"...Yes. You?" I answered a bit late, when another song came on and he was jammin' it out in his seat.

"Cant you tell?" He yelled.
I Just Wanna Run, The Downtown Fiction.

"I just wanna run, hide it away!" He sang.

Sooner best than later we got to that narrow street, with the wide fence and no houses and with trees. Wesley was the one who lowered the volume and we caught sight of it all. I drove slowly, trying to give us both a little peace of mind for a second. But it was inevitable. The road ended about two minutes later and Wesley was just as surprised as I was to see this street..., boring here. The shock was only temporary, then he turned it up and kept having fun next to me. My little brother, Wesley. Sometimes it doesn't feel as though he's my brother at all, but my other half. He completes me and I hate to seem like if he means the world to me, but he does. Sometimes he just seems more than my brother, like my medicine that keeps me alive. The medicine I love to see every day and night and any time in between.

My Wesley Medicine, I can't get enough.

Honk, honk! Honk, honk, honk, honk, honk!

Justin was at the door then. He seemed to have difficulties as he tried to get outside. He was struggling with something that was hiding behind the wall. His gaze went down to the floor. His leg looked like it was being held on to. But by what?

He in the end got free and walked to the car as though nothing had happened. He opened the door behind me and got in.

"So...? Let's do this." A very cheery Justin said from behind me.

I pulled out of his driveway, noticing that everywhere I look there were no kids around. There were no toys left outside or even adults coming out of their homes in pajamas to get the mail. There were just houses and driveways and little trees in front of most of the houses. The way to the gellateria wasn't very complex for me. I always used to take Wes and sometimes Bobo there, walking. The magic road came in sight to us and it was really a treat. It was just so wonderful and peaceful. It's like if nothing could ever go wrong here.

At the end of our trip I think Wes was about ready to eat half of everything in sight. He was pretty happy and Justin seemed happy, too. We got out of the car and ran inside where it was too hot to be an actual ice-cream store.

There were two people in front of the line that we were in.

"What do you want?" Justin asked Wesley.
"I can pay." I informed him.
"...Or I can pay." He told me.
I smiled and nodded no. I didn't really felt like arguing with him anytime soon right now.

"A medium strawberry ice-cream with a cherry on top." Wesley told him.
"Alright. Al, what do you want?" He asked me.
"...I don't want anything." I looked out of the window.
"I'm sure you do. Come on, we don't have all day."
"Actually, I'm driving, so yes we do." I told him.
"Just get something," Said a little kid from behind me. "It's not killing you to get ice-cream."
"Thank you." Justin agreed with him.
"...Fine, I'll take what Wesley is taking."
"Fine, much better." Justin said.
Such a big deal for ice-cream; is it so hard to not get ice cream if you don't want it?

We were eating our ice-cream in the car at this point. Justin got a strawberry banana split without the banana. 30 Seconds to Mars were playing The Kill in the radio. I would sing-a-long with them, but I was trying to eat the ice-cream really fast so I had enough time to sing-a-long. Justin and Wes apparently were looking at me as I tried to devour it down. I was pretty late to join in.

"Hungry?" Justin asked.

"...Forget it." I told him.

"This is so *awesome*!" I heard Wes yell from inside of the car when I went to go and throw away my cup.

When I came back the boys were laughing away about something.

"I told you; 'leave it like that.'" Wesley told him.

"You were right, bud." Justin agreed from behind.

"Huh?" I asked.

"...The car. Justin wanted it red. I told him told him to leave it black. You imagine this baby...***red***?" Wes laughed.

"Why red? I mean I like red, but not on this car." I said.

"Wes was a huge help fixing up the car."

"Hey! Holding that flash light was a hard job." Wes argued.

'Holding the flash light?' I asked myself.

I wonder if dad would be proud, proud that his car was handed down into my hands, my good hands. If he's proud that Wes helped Justin fix his dream car up to make me happy. I wonder if he is proud of us, of us just being together. Whatever it might be, I think dad would be proud. Dad always did like it when Wes and I teamed up. So, would he like it if Wes and Justin teamed up this time? Oh, the questions, the questions. Unanswered they shall be.

After our little rest, Wes told us that it would be fun if we went to the park. It was a stupid idea to think that we could go to the park in this weather. But, we did go to the park. And we did have fun even if it was pretty cold out. I took Justin home after that. He thanked us and Wes and I headed home. Having a car is so liberating to me. I have more freedom than what I used to. No one can stop me from just hanging out with my little brother in my car. Even when Wesley grows up I doubt that I will past down   the car to him. I love this car and I love Wes too, but this car means too much to me to let it fall in potentially dangerous hands. The drive home was quiet, but peaceful. Wes turned the volume of the car down a bit. He still rocked to the songs he knew, but at a lower volume.

"Mom!" I yelled from the door.

"I'll go take a shower." Wesley told me as he past me by on his way up the stairs.

"Mom, where are you!" I yelled again.

It was seconds that went by, and then I went to check on Bobo. It was minutes that pasted by and I realized that Bobo wasn't in his crib. It was more minutes that went by when I realized that no one else seemed to be home. Mom was still on house arrest, so she shouldn't have gone far.

'Where's John?'

I looked into mom's room. There's no one there, but dirty laundry all over the place. John should have cleaned this place up. Or at lease he should have told Seashell to do it. I walked all over that floor, looking for Bobo. I could hear Wesley singing in the shower. There was still no sign of him after about five minutes. There was no sign of mom after about five minutes. There was still no sign John after about five minutes. I was worried. Did John and mom runaway, taking Bobo with them? They couldn't have. John knows better. But mom doesn't.

When I got home today I *never* expected to find the house empty. I could've never expected that something like this would happen. It was something *completely* unexpected... and scary.

I ran outside. I looked everywhere; the backyard, the garage, the front yard, the neighbors' yard. They weren't there. I cried. I sat on our porch...and I cried. I might be held responsible and I should. I should have known that leaving Bobo with mom was a terrible idea. The woman went naked running around the streets once. Bobo was in danger and if something happens to him... I don't know how I'll manage. I cried there, my face in my hands, my shame completely showing. Wesley came out shortly after that. He wrapped me with his hands and he laid his head on my shoulder.

"I lost them." I said after awhile.

"...We lost them." He isn't making all of this easier.

My entire life I've kept him out of trouble and I liked it. Now, technically, I've made him get in trouble. What if the cops came to our home? What if Seashell's patrol officer comes by? What happens if she get's caught?

'Bobo.' Will they take him, too, a baby? Will they take him to some orphanage? Will I still see him, or take care of him?

'Wes.' Nothing can happen to Wesley, absolutely nothing. 'I'm so sorry, Wes.' I should have stayed home and watched over them. Maybe then nothing wrong would have happened.

Wesley took me inside and laid me on the couch. He told me that he would fix me up some soup and that everything will work out. But how, how could he even be so sure? I laid there, watching TV, thinking about a solution to this catastrophic problem. If anything does happen to *us* thanks to *them*, I'll find a way to leave Wesley off the hook. It wasn't his fault. Not in my eyes. In my eyes Wesley was just trying to have a little fun before going back to school on Monday. Leaving home this morning didn't seem like such a bad idea then as it does now.

When Wes came in with the finished soup, he started to feed it to me as he sat on the floor. I heard him whispering things to me. He was supporting me, telling me how every little thing's gonna work out just fine. A few tears came down... and he...

Wes looked at me and he cleaned my cheeks. He kissed my forehead and stood up. He left the soup on the dinning room table and walked away. I didn't look at him; I was losing myself in the TV. I wanted to because it was a distraction.

"Yes, yes. Thank you." I heard Wesley say into the phone when they were giving commercials.

"...Wes?" I asked in my weak voice, I didn't have the strengths. "Who was that?" I forced it out.

"...I called for help."

"... Who?"

"The cops." He said, he sounded so...brave.

I wondered why he would do that. Did I seem as though I was too weak to do anything? I didn't want to feel as if Wesley would need to count on other people more than me. He called the police...because I seemed too weak to handle anything at this   point, and in some way this was somewhat true. I was weak. Maybe even too weak to try and find them anymore. But if was true.

'Have I disappointed Wes? Have I disappointed dad?'

The kind of mess that I'm in could not be fixed so easily. I wanted answers and I wanted to feel good enough again, but it was not easy. Mom has taken Bobo, knowing she's on house arrest! John perhaps took them somewhere, to make a family of his own and he probably wants Bobo as his own now. I just don't know where they could be. I searched and searched this place; if they are anywhere they are not here.

"How do I look to you, Wes?" I asked.
Wesley walked closer to me and sat on the floor.

"You look like if you can't take it anymore. It's probably my fault. I've hardly *ever* said thank you to you for every little thing you do for me. I'm sorry. I'll fix this, it was my fault. You just rest."

"...Wes!" I shouted, and he flinched. "You're just suppose to be the kid here, I'm suppose to fix things and make it easy for you."

"Owlina Misty Parker!" Wes said? "You have done *nothing but* that ever since dad died, years ago! I'm helping! You're not stopping me! I'll get things fixed up and we'll continue our lives." My little brother, "Rest!" He ordered.

"... Wesley...," I couldn't argue. "Don't do anything stupid."

"...I'm not a little kid anymore, AL." He kissed my cheek and pointed.

I nodded and he left the house.

It was true; Wesley wasn't a little kid anymore. He's fifteen. But he's my little brother and he'll always be that. I don't have issues facing that. I just hoped that this day wouldn't come, the day when Wesley became Wes.

I fell asleep. I heard a car pull up into the driveway as my conscious faded.

The town of Short Rainbows came up into my view. Lollipop Lucy came skipping to me in her Saturday Light blue clothes and greeted me. I said hi to her and she beamed with happiness. Rainbow Roanna, the queen of Short Rainbows, came to us with a sad face. I've never seen her anything but happy. I knew that this couldn't be good. Everyone else came walking behind her, all heading towards us. Cookie Dough

Carry, Shorty Short Stacks, Quackery Questions Quinn, Pinhead Peanut Peter, Banana Bob, Little Lighting Lucile, and even Angry Anchovies Alvin came to us. The whole town was there, Lollipop Lucy at my side was getting worried. I asked her what was this about and she assured that she didn't know.

"All Loopy Al, I have terrible news for you." Rainbow Roanna told me.

I curtsied and she tried smile at me. When I straightened myself I could see that everyone behind her, including her, wore sad faces upon their adorable selves.

"What is going on, Rainbow Roanna?" Lollipop Lucy asked her.

"I'm afraid that you must leave Short Rainbows." She answered her but was looking at me.

"...Me?" I asked, "But why? I haven't done anything wrong." I vouched.

"But indeed you have." She said with a warm smiled. Sarcasm winded through me. "You have done this place wrong."

"How?" I begged for an answer on my knees.

"If you would have never gotten that car, and driven it today, than maybe Bobo would still be here. I can not give you another try after something like this. I'm sorry, but you must leave Short Rainbows and never come back. You may go anywhere else, but not here. Leave at once and take your things. I am sorry, but when something like this happens I must take charge to protect my kingdom. Do you understand?" She looked down at me.

I was sitting on the floor. Lollipop Lucy was trying to comfort me. I nodded my head and leaned it down. *My* kingdom was *vanishing* me from it, forever. I had done something wrong. I had lost one of our own.

Lollipop Lucy helped me to my feet and hugged me. Every one of my friends came running to hug me as well. After that I headed home and packed a bag. Then Lollipop Lucy helped me to carry it. We went back to where we received the terrible news and Rainbow Roanna stood in front of us once more. She lifted her right hand and touched my forehead with two of her fingers. I heard Lollipop Lucy whispering goodbye. Everything went pitch white, fast. I had heard a loud pitch sound, then it faded away…, and then I woke up.

I opened my eyes to find that it was beginning to become dark out. I looked around me as I sat up. There was no one in the room besides me. The TV was turned off and I believe I heard sounds coming from the other room. When I stood up I took the plate of soup and went to kitchen to 'dirt free' it up. After that I went outside to check if   anyone was there. Surprisingly, it wasn't as cold as before. I wasn't feeling any better either. My car was there in the driveway, the grass wasn't moving, the porch was still as I had left it, and yet something felt different. I went back inside and went upstairs, to check if they have come home. I checked Wesley's room first. Bobo's crib was still empty. Wes had fallen asleep in his. I walked up to him and kissed his face, and he wiggled a little bit in his bed and then calmed down. I left him to go and check in other rooms. There was no noise, no movement, no mom or John in their room. I checked the bathroom and the only thing that was there was the horrible stench coming from the trashcan. I went in my room, just to be sure. Nothing.

'I'm toast. NO, I'm more than toast…, I'm squashed.'

I went back downstairs. I felt bad. Bobo's life could be in danger here, and I can't think of one thing to do. So, I just went to get to my jacket and I went to my car. It was warmer in here, not temperature related though. I felt love in my car. A nice warm feeling, I estimate it as love. I like this feeling. I then soon turned on my radio and leaned back. I was trying to relax. Something like this has not *ever* happen before. Like if your baby falls from the crib for the first time, you'd be worried if you loved your baby. Or like if a best friend gets fit by a car, you'd be worried. My mom and Bobo are missing, for the first time, and I'm worried. Relaxing seems like the only thing that made sense around here. He was nice to me. He let me in and he let me seat on his seat. He let me hear music on his radio and he let me relax inside of him. The car loves me. As crazy as it may sound, he loves me. That was the love, warming feeling that I was feeling; it came from him.

At around nine-thirty, I got out of my car and went back. Wesley was eating something. I believe that he mixed some mashed potatoes and some whip cream to make some kind of toping to his ice cream. I didn't see any cherry so I just figured that he'd eaten it first.

"Are you hungry?" I asked him as I walked closer to him.

He took his glaze off from his food and looked up at me with a little smile.

"A little."

"I can make something if you want." I told him.

"...I can take care of that. You keep resting." He then looked back at his "food."

"...How, Wes?" You can't underestimate Wesley, but I unfortunately do it a lot more than what I should.

"Remember I called the cops?"

"But, Wes. What if they send mom to jail, and what about Bobo? Can't they send him to some orphanage or something? They can take him away from us, we did something wrong." I felt guilty.

"...You say we did something wrong and I just say that it was one out of many. It's just another mistake, problem, we'll fix."

"Wesley, stop it. I'll take care of it."

He was silent for a moment and he stood up from his seat with anger. He looked at me and then he tossed his cup of ice cream to the floor with a push of his hand. He showed anger and rage in his eyes.

"Would you stop!? This arguing isn't helping, you know?" He looked down on the mess he'd made, and then continued. "You don't have to think that you are doing this on your own, Al. I'm here." He looked back at me then. "I always have and you haven't let me help. Bobo is my brother too, and mom is my mother, too. I will help and you can't stop me."

"I won't stop you, Wes. I just want you to realize that I can handle it myself." I told him.

"No, you can't. You've handled enough. I called the cops, because I thought they can help to find them. What does it matter where they send them as long as we know where they are?" He said. He was right.

"...You're right. You're not that idiotic little brother I used to have." I told him.

Even though the police was something that I didn't wanted to get involved, they could help. And thanks to Wesley I now know that. I sat on the couch, letting Wes feed me some more soup. I wonder why Wesley thinks that soup can fix a person so much that he would feed it to me so much.

"Why do you feed me soup?" I asked his in-between one spoonful of soup.

He smiled.

"You fed me soup nonstop back when I was like super little and would get sick. Mom did too when she was normal."

"...I remember. You were some little thing. You never went an entire season *without* getting sick."

"Yeah, but you...and this soup where here."

"I always hated one soup I gave Bobo, some kind of vegetable soup. I hated it. Mom fed it to me once, before dad died, I throw up right after I was finished. 'All of that for nothing', I thought."

"I never had it."

"And hopefully you never will."

We spend the rest of that time talking about the past, the past with dad in it. Like when dad took me and Wes to go to a 30 Seconds to Mars concert. After the concert he took us to this bar, he had too much and threw up. Dad said that it was intentionally and healthy to throw up. It was a fun night. Wes and I went and played Pictionary for the rest of the night. Something in me believed that things were going to work out. I think that the only thing that really bothered me was that I didn't know how. I was proud of Wesley. He'd convinced me that I don't have to do things on my own and that he's not that little boy anymore. That he's growing up and he can take care of things, as well. I guess that just because dad told me to take care of Wesley and I should do it, for as long as possible I guess. But he's older now, and even if I still wanted to he wouldn't let me help. He'd have me resting. I guess that now is really the time when he starts repaying me for all of the good I've done to him. For all of the protection I've served him. For all of the love I've showed him. Wes is still my little brother... and I still want that vision of mine in the Wichita Mountains with Wes. I'm still not sure if Bobo is going to be with us... or even if mom's going to get better and take care Bobo. I just hope my senses turned upside right and that it's true that things are truly going to get better than this...or better than before.

The next thing I know its Monday and I hear Wes knocking on my door to wake up. It's hilarious to think that Wes could actually wake up first than me. I took my time in the shower, but tried to hurry to get dressed and to go eat something. Wes apparently had made scramble eggs. He looked adorable in his school uniform. It seemed as though I'd last seen him in it years go, instead of days. I took us to school and parked in the students' parking lot. It was cool parking with the others' cars, but mine was the best one there, hands down. School seemed like if I'd never gone to it...at all, like if it's been five months at least.

I walked in through the front doors with Wes next to me. I felt ridiculous, wearing uniform that didn't look remotely close to something that I'd wear, and I was in school when I was supposed to be out looking for Bobo and mom and John. What's John's problem anyway? It's not like him to just take off and not even let me know of   where   he   or mom or Bobo've gone. Either way, I guess that what I have to focus on now is school. I was good at dealing with different circumstances and focusing on one thing, though this was different. This had to do with my legally insane mother, my gorgeous half-baby-brother, and my not-so-stupid step-father. Wes was in it, too. He was what I might loose for acting stupid, and imprudent, and...completely mental. I felt extremely bad the more I thought about it. I took my time going through the metal detector and going into the cafeteria took a lot out of me. I stopped at the cafeteria entrance, I looked down and I just stayed there. I could feel the tens of looks that stopped at me, and I just didn't really want to see any of them. I had no idea what could've prevented this tragedy from happening. Wes's hand touched my back at that point. I couldn't continue my thoughts because, well, I'll come back to life in half a second if it meant that Wesley, Wes, needed me. I saw a smile peeking out of his lips as he slowly shook his head.

"They're serving chicken soup now. Go eat some, you'll sit wit me today." He told me.

I looked inside of the room, where I could see every single person in my sight, they *were* looking at me. Wes pushed a little, but in a good way. I could see the freshmen to my left. They all just huddled together, little penguins. I felt bad for them, because it's hard to even move. The security guard makes everyone move inside of the cafeteria in the morning, there are a lot of kids here, but seeing this... It's insane, I should know. There was enough space near the wall to my right to get in the line for breakfast, while Wes went and sat with his two friends. I always see this girl going up to him. She reminds me a little of Aria, in the looks department. Though, let's hope that she's absolutely nothing like Ariadne. Though, I think she means well, because Aria just doesn't seem trustworthy enough yet. I hope this girl is. The line was long, and my patience boiled up and exploded at times, in the time I was in that line.

I waited and waited and waited for that line to move. It took forever for one kid to just get some ketchup, because apparently the bag *had* to be clean and nice and sealed tight before he could open it. Unfortunately, just some minutes before, it sounded like, some special kid came and opened one of those little ketchups and spilled it all over the others. So, yes, it took forever for just that one kid to go and get his meal. I would have probably yelled and cursed at him if he was mom. Not that I don't like mom, it's just how I naturally think that I should be with her. I think of trying to be nice to her, and again...it's really just plain and wrong. I took that soup and tried to get to where Wes was without asking anyone to move out of my way. I wasn't one hundred percent sure, but my voice wasn't good today. Wes's friends looked dead at me when I was pulling out a chair. I was super sure that Wes looked at them as if he was going to kill them if they didn't stop. I set next to him and he watched me as I ate every single spoonful of that soup.

"What?" I asked him.

"I just want to make sure you eat it all. There must be some reason why you're not getting any better."

"...It's only been about a day, Wes. Give it...," I eat some more. "Some time, Wes."

His friends looked at each other, and I was too busy focusing on my soup that I couldn't catch what face they made to each other. I would ask them for their names and try to become friends with them, but I couldn't see the point to that. They didn't seem to like me much and I wasn't going to just change a little to have some of my brother's friends like me. I really just didn't see the function to it. After I ate all of my soup, I went and cleaned up after myself. I saw Wes and his friends standing up from their table as I came back. Wes pointed to the door as he tried to have me look at him. There were a lot of people pushing and yelling at each other to move, so I tried my best to understand what Wes was pointed to. When I got to the exit, I made my way down the hall and to my locker. I saw familiar faces on my way there. They all seemed to have wanted to hug me hello, but why? I couldn't see the purpose on that either. Why bother hugging you hello if I will see you tomorrow and all of the hugging will just be routine? Why bother saying hello to you now if there is plenty of time in the time that we see each other to say hello? It just felt like something stupid that Seashell would do. Something stupid that I had to yell at someone for, to let them know that it's wrong. In this case it was nonsense.

Wes was at my locker when I got there. He told me to look out and be careful, and to try not to fall down or loose my balance while he's not around.

I went to my first period class and thought to myself...

'I'm going to have to at least try to get through this.' Would I have to do this for the rest of the week? This scared me. What if I cracked and I just began to yell at random people in the halls? I wasn't sure how long I would endeavor to go through this, but if Wes tried than I guess it wouldn't really hurt me to take it step by step and try to go through today first, rather than think about Tuesday, Wednesday, and Thursday, and Friday. If the cops   did have anything by then, then I would have to keep going. Saturday, Sunday, then my torture began all over again.

I was cursing everything on my way there, to get everything out now I mean. I cursed the stupid lockers for being so ridiculously small. The stupid trash cans were next, they should be recycling bins! The stupid floor was so ugly and stupid and ridiculously stupid for being here! Why the hell would you be here? Why don't you just break and leave this freaking horror place, you insane piece of tile! I can't believe all of these things have ways out of here..., I don't. I have months more to go before I can ever go. These...*things* can break in less than a second and they could be free. Where's the point in staying if you're miserable? Where's the point in me staying when I got a car to leave in?

"Welcome back, everyone!" Said my way too-excited-to-be-a-teacher, Mrs. Figs. "Sit, sit! I'll wait a bit longer for everyone to get here though. In the meantime, why don't *you* guys start on a simple bell work assignment to refresh your memory? Let's see...hmm."

She got this thinking look on her face as she looked around the class. There were only seven of us here now and she was looking at us back and forward. I probably was the only one to notice, too. "...Chrystal...and Dan, please pass the papers?" She asked as she handed them each a pile of papers.

I think I was doing pretty good, considering... Mrs. Figs sat in her chair and began to write something on some greenish book of hers. I tried. This bell work seemed like if it was written in Japanese and I wasn't Japanese. I turned it around and put down my pencil on the table. I laid my head down and closed my eyes. I couldn't go back to Short Rainbows. I woke up and killed my chances of ever returning.

The rest of the day went on, and by sixth period I was about to spring a leak. That tape that was there wasn't strong enough from stopping the crack..., but then...

"Hey..." Said some worried person in front of my desk. My face was looking at my English book, trying to read some assigned story, for some reason.

I lifted up my head and smiled when my vision caught sight of something...nice. For the first time in a while... something nice came around. Wes doesn't count, because he's always around and always nice.

"... Hi, Jaystin."

"Good morning," He said it a bit...slowly, almost unsure, I think.

"...What?" I asked after a while, he'd been checking my face out.

"You look **terrible**." He said with wide eyes. His face went back to normal as he took his seat next to me.

It took me a little bit to realize that he'd cut his hair. It used to be up to his ears or a bit pass that. Now, it's as long as any normal boy's hair. I felt kind of bad that he'd cut his hair.

"Why?" I asked.

He smiled and answered..., "For my job."

I would ask him why his job required for him to cut his hair or why he didn't just quit that job and he wouldn't have to cut his hair? But, I stayed silent, waiting for him to pick up our next subject.

"So, might I ask why do you look so terrible?" He asked. "Almost makes me want to throw up." He added a bit softly.

I thought about it in my mind for a second or two. I would tell Justin about this weekend because of the fact that I can trust him. I wouldn't tell Justin because of the fact that it hurt too much to think about it.

"Saturday," I told him.

He got this thoughtful look in his face, but I think he still wanted me to go on.

"We come home and no one's home." Ouch!

Justin's face went from thoughtful to sad, from sad to examining something..., to blank.

"Bobo?" He asked.

"Gone." I said softly. "Mom and John are too. I haven't heard anything from the cops ever since Saturday, but I didn't hear anything from them on Saturday either."

"...What do you mean?" H asked.

"...Wes said he'll take care of it. I fell asleep, but I managed to hear a car pull into the driveway before I completely fell asleep."

"...I'm *so* sorry." He whispered.

Mr. Looby came walking down the row to my left. Justin, on my right, took out his English book from under his desk and opened it. Mr. Looby might have noticed something, I don't know what. It could have been that someone farted or even that he hear a ten pound meatball fall down to the floor in the cafeteria, but I could tell from his face he saw, or felt, something different. When he walked away I couldn't take school anymore.

So, I just closed my book and laid down my head. I tried to nap for as long as I could to help me out, but it wasn't enough. According to Justin I was asleep for thirty minutes before he'd waken me up so that I could write down the homework. After the bell rang I head for Calculus. I wasn't looking forward to it, but I do love Calculus. Maybe this class would make me feel better. I would never truly know until I get my butt into that class.

I told Mr. Leto that I wasn't up for any jokes or really hard stuff today and he nodded his head yes with a simple worried look that covered his face. I took my seat in the second row in the second column. Justin sat in the fifth column in the first seat. I opened my notebook and got my pencil out. I took a simple glance at the bell work and my head was already hurting. I heard someone calling me from behind and I tried to turn around to see who it was.

"Hi, Shortness!" Said... Kevin.

I beamed a smile at him and waved hello. It didn't hurt to smile to Kevin because it's just naturally easy to be in a good mood around him, even if he was about four seats behind me. Kevin makes me laugh and smile, mostly smile. Seth makes me laugh, and laugh, and laugh until it hurts. He seats next to me in one of our computer classes and though he and my computer deserve a good slap, I still love how he makes me laugh so much.

"How are you?" He asked.

I could clearly see that it was only about six other people who were looking at us talking, besides Mr. Leto. Either some were talking to other kids, or about two of them were actually trying to do the bell work, or they were just practicing their skills in making paper airplanes.

"...How are you?" I tried to avoid the question by asking the same question. Or by answering with the same question, to me it's kind of ingenious.

"HA-HA!" He laughed. "I'm good, good. I just got my sweater back from Jasmine. You?"

Jasmine was sitting one seat next to me and one seat forward.

"...I...got a car." It was the only good news that came to mind.

"No way!" He acted surprised. He really was, but in his own soft-voice-excited way. "Take me for a ride some day?" He begged.

"Most definitely." I said.

After I finished that sentence I could hear Mr. Leto trying to quiet everyone down from behind me. He went to the chalkboard and wrote, "Talk and you'll be sorry," with a little crying face beneath it. I saw Kevin mouth the word okay and I turned around to try and do the bell work. Simple enough that even I should be able to do. Once Calculus was over I head to my locker. I *was* feeling better. As I tried to open it, I realized that Kevin was following me. He stopped right next to me and started talking,

"So, what's new?"

"...Besides...the car...I'm not too..., too sure." I stuttered.

"HA-HA! Funny. You are too funny." He patted my head like if I was a little dog. "Well, okay then, don't want to be late for lunch or anything, right?"

'It's lunchtime already?'

"...Right." I said once I'd realized that he was waiting there for an actual answer.

He was laughing for a little while as he walked away. I love his blue eyes. They are really, really blue. I've never said this before but...you really can get lost in his eyes. Oh, Kevin.

I always go to the line closest to the door. I usually catch sight of Damion and Steve. They're like the school's gods or something. Steve *usually* is in line a few people in front of me and by the time I head down to lunch Damion already has his lunch. My only girl friends I don't really pay much attention to them, only about two get exceptions.

It always does take a while to get my lunch. I would go to the other line since it is faster, but there's just something that prevents me. When I got to my seat there already were kids there, most of them were my classmates. Jasmine always sits at the far end while I sit on the other side on the end. I noticed this girl looking at me as I   unwrapped my burger. She was sitting right in front of me on the other table. The second time I looked up at her she signaled to go over there, I didn't hesitate. I sat on the sit in front of her and she began to talk about the new security guard the school got. She asked me if I thought that he was either Puerto Rican or White. I told her that he could be mixed and that he looked mighty delicious. I don't even know her name, but I've seen her around school, so she's not a total stranger. I left a little after that and went to continue my food.

Wes then comes through the cafeteria doors and starts looking around. Then I see him rushing toward me and he leans over to make sure I can hear him.

"How are you?" He asks.
"...Fine. I'm hungry." I said in-between bites.
"..." He kissed the top of my head and went back to his position. "I need you to be careful." He said softly.
"...I'm fine, Wes, really."
"I know you are, because I'm going to make sure of that."

The next thing I know Wes went to go and talk to Damion who was at a different table behind me across the room.

"What's that all about?" Asked my friend Alex sitting next to me.

I turned to look at him and I shrugged my shoulders.

"...Brothers." I said, then returning my attention to Wesley.

Damion and Wes both look back at me and I froze. When Wes seemed like he was done Damion nodded his head and let Wes go.

"What was that?" I asked nervously and curiously.

He didn't even smile. He took my head in both of his hands and kissed the top of my head again.

"Eat." He said.

He left me to wonder. I could just wait until computer class and ask Damion what Wes wanted, but I wouldn't want him to think that I'm a worrywart or anything like that.

It was soon ninth period and I head to the computer class with Seth and Damion in it. Justin doesn't have this class, he goes somewhere else and we meet up some other time.

"You wanna know a secret?" Seth's first words to me were before I could sit down.

"...Sure." I said as I logged into the computer.

"...You're my best friend. Al, you're so funny. My favorite color's orange." He whispered.

"...Thanks, Seth. You're like super funny, too." I said slowly.

I noticed Damion come in just then. He sits across the room and two computers down on the first row, next to Ben.

"Welcome back, guys." Said teach. "Open up your pages and we'll get started." She said when the bell rang.

"Ms." Ben raised his hand. "How much is our next work going to be?"

"A lot." She warned.

"And can I get extra credit or something, before the semester ends?"

"...Just finish all of the work you haven't finished and make sure I grade it." She smiled.

"Sugar poop!" Seth cried from behind me.

"What?" I asked.

"Your shoe brushed off my pants." Seth cried out. "I'm going to cry. No, I'm going to tell on you." He raised his hand and stopped when he realized that I wasn't playing around with him right now. "What's wrong?" He asked.

"...I'm sorry." I began to clean his pants for him.

He stopped me and got serious. It's always strange when Seth becomes serious.

"Al?" He said.

"...What?" I kept cleaning.

"Stop..., stop." He whispered.

When I did I saw that everyone was looking at me. Jasmine was the first to start laughing. I blushed a little bit and went back to work, pretending like nothing happened. I could feel Damion looking at me. I wanted to look, but I didn't want to. I thought that he'd think something bad of me. At the end of *that* class Damion waiting a few feet away from the door. He looked at what seemed to be nothing. As I passed him to go to class I felt really nervous.

"Al!" He yelled after a few...seconds.

He rushed to my side and I stopped walking and turned to face him.

"Hey." He said.

"... Hi."

"...You okay?" He asked.

I nodded and said, "Yes."

"... Good, good. Do you need help with anything..., you know, I can help."

"...What does Wes want from you?" I didn't think of how it should come out, it just did.

"..." He hesitated. "He wants me to take care of you." He said.

"...And what do you get?"

"..." He blushed and said, "Nothing," shamefully.

"The bell's about to ring." Said...Kevin, a few minutes later.

Damion said goodbye and went up the stairs to... class I suppose. I walked with Kevin to class. He was telling me about his little three-year-old brother and how cute and smart he is. I competed against him by telling him about my two-year-old baby cousin and how I taught her how to fist punch and high-five. He almost got me when he said that his brother had his eyes. When we sat down I told him that my cousin was growing up with gray eyes and he said...

"...You win." Aunt Karen is extremely gorgeous so it's no wonder.

School was about ready to be over and I was feeling bunches better thanks to Kevin, who for today sat next to me. He started asking questions about some drama situations in school involving me and two other people. I told him the truth and somehow we ended up leaving the class joking about one of the people. Apparently, he didn't like her either, which increases my admiration towards Kevin. I told him how bad we were being and he called her a pig. In truth, she was, she even looks like one.

So, I waited for Wesley by the front doors. When he did show, he was with Justin. They were laughing and having a good-old-time coming down the three flights of stairs.

"...Yup, and I'm not even kidding about that last part either." Wes told him.

"That's epic, Wes!" Justin admired.

"...Ready?" Wes asked.

I nodded.

"Let's go than." Wes urged.

We walked a parking lot to get to my car. My car. I still can't believe it. After we were all in and set to go, Wes turned on the radio and 30 Seconds to Mars were singing This Is War. I turned it up louder and got strange looks as reactions from Wes and Justin.

"Feeling better?" Justin asked when I was pulling out of the parking lot.

"... It's the moment of truth and the moment to lie and the moment to live and the moment to die." I turned my head to make sure no one was looking and I started to drive away, "The moment to fight to fight to fight." I sang.

Wesley nodded his head yes back at Justin and they laughed together again.

"So, am I taking you home?" I asked Justin once the song was over.

"... Oh, no. He's helping us." Wes answered.

"...With what?"

"Finding Bobo and Seashell and John." Justin replied.

"...The cops are on it." I said, only I could tell that I wasn't sure.

"It's been three days, two, whatever. You don't think that someone should have found something by now?" Wes asked.

I'm done thinking about this.

I drove to Justin's house and he was shy as he left the car. Wesley fought with me that Justin should stay. I refused and drove home. Wes seemed to still be mad at me by the time we got there. There still wasn't any sight of any of the three's survival inside.

I didn't even bother to try and talk to Wes anymore. I took my backpack and headed upstairs to go and do my homework in peace. It was around seven-something when I was finished. I went downstairs and there they were; Bobo in mom's hands; mom under John's arm;   and John standing in front of the door. I didn't process anything. I ran and snatched Bobo from her hands and I ran to the living room, where Wes was laying down, watching TV.

"I will kill you!" I threatened.

Wes stood up so fast that I didn't realize when he'd gotten to my side.

"Al?" He asked.

"I will shoot you!" I warned them.

They just stood there. John had barely flinched and mom wasn't even listening.

"Stop, Al. Calm down." Wes soothed.

He rubbed my shoulders in an attempt to calm me down.

"Al, listen. Listen to me. Shake your head if you are listening." He instructed.

I hesitated a second later.

"The cops came in a while ago, looking for you, but I thought you were asleep. They spent a night in jail for breaking rules. Seashell only got one day because...she's crazy." He'd said the last part kind of fast. "The point is...they're back. Can we calm down and talk about this? Al, come on."

"No." I roared...at them not at Wesley.

"Then listen..." John said.

"Shut up." I said.

"Al, they took Bobo and didn't want to come back. They were headed to...some cave. The police found them walking from some motel...the same day." He was telling me all of this as if the last parts didn't really matter. "They caught them and these *morons* told them who they are. Luckily for us they did. They had to stay in prison for some time and now they have a court trial for their little behavior in a few months." He finished with a smile that signified that the information wasn't important.

"Owlina." Mom said with open arms.

Wesley stood in-between us and told her not to touch me, I smiled. John stood there just watching everything go down.

"Owlina, come on." She was drunk. "It was JUST a simple prank. It was a Joke!" She shifted from side to side.

John then came and placed her back under his arm and said *nothing*. She was giggling and hiccupping until Wes talked.

"You all are crazy! Why the hell would you even *want* to take Bobo, John!? He's not *you're* son!" Wes barked. "You should have known better! The fuck were *you* thinking?" He yelled at Seashell.

She started to cry and John comforted her.

After a little while the only thing that was there was the sound of Seashell's crying.

"I'm getting a *huge* bonus from work in no time. We," I pointed to Wes, Bobo, and me, "are leaving this shit." I said. "I've had enough. I've *tried* to be nice to you, but it's always felt...useless, a waste of time, inevitable that we *have* to go. You are a work of shit, bitch." I told her. "And you're the bitch's bitch." I told John.

Wes laughed and took Bobo in his arms. Bobo got really excited, with his amazingly cute two teeth showing. I told Wes to go and move his bed and Bobo's crib into my room; it's the only room with a lock. I walked over and bumped them on my way upstairs. I went to go and get the house phone from out of Wes's room and went into my room.

Dialing a number to go and talk to someone felt pathetic..., but it felt right. I dialed Kirsten's number. She's been my friend since second grade. She left Phlox a pretty long time ago and moved to Nier. It's about a hundred miles or so from here. She'd told me to keep in touch, but I guess I'd taken that as to only call her when I needed her.

"Hello?" A strange cracking voice said from the other side.

"...Hello? Is Kirsten home?" I asked.

"Yes. Who's this?" It asked.

"...Al." I hesitated.

"...Al?" There was a short silence. The static seemed pretty loud to me. "AL! Oh my Lord! Owlina Misty Parker! How have you been? It's been **way** too long. Why haven't you called? You should call more often, we miss having you around, toots."

Toots. Only one person in this entire planet would dare call me Owlina and Toots and get away with it.

"Nice to hear from you too, Mrs. Adams."

"Well, Sweet Cheeks, let me go and get Kirsten out for you. Also, sorry about my voice; it's the middle of autumn here and I'm afraid it's not treating me so well."

"I'm...sorry to hear that."

"Again, it's just a little cold." She stopped talking again. "Al..., I'm sorry about your father. Please tell Wesley to stay out of trouble and to always leave his house with a belt. Lord only knows how long ago it was until that boy learned how to use a belt."

"Yes, ma'am." I said.

"Very well, give me a second, Sweetie."

"Bye, Mrs. Adams."

It was probably two minutes later that I heard a soft, sweet, child-like voice coming from the other line.

"Al..., is that really you?"

"...Yes. Hi, Kirsten."

"Ooh, my!" She whispered. "Al, do you realize how long it's been? It's been years! More than five, eight, I tell yah! Why didn't you call sooner! There's been *so much* that I had to tell you!"

"Why didn't you call me?"

"I lost your number when we moved. The first house had mice and dad apparently was allergic. We moved to a bigger and nicer home without mice. The move took days and days. I tried not to loose anything, but your number was the only thing I lost. Well, really I lost my entire phonebook."

"...Mom ran away with Bobo on Saturday. We just found them."

"...What! Al..., who's Bobo?" She was shocked.

"My... Mom had another kid with some guy at a bar one day. She had Bobo and well, it wasn't long until she got arrested, house arrested."

"Owlina, I am really upset with you now. How dare you not call me in those times!? I really don't know why you even bothered to keep my number if you will only call years later after serious things had happened!" It sounded as if she was about to cry, but for me. "Last time you called it was after *your father died*. Al, please just do us all a favor and don't dare call only once every nine years."

"I'm sorry. I just thought you might be having too much fun over there and I didn't want to be a burden."

"Being a burden is different than not having any contact with them at all, Owlina." She was quiet. "Tell me what's wrong."

I didn't hold anything back. I told every single thing I could think of. From all of the things that happened with Wes, to mom, to Justin and Ariadne. From memories and dreams I've had about dad, to me getting my license and dad's car. I told her about how Justin might have been a father to Penny. I wasn't prepared to hear what *she* had to tell *me*.

"Penny's my girlfriend. She actually asked me to marry her not long ago. She's my fiancée."

It was hard to think that we were really talking about the same Penelope. Ariadne has told me plenty about her, and Justin never talked about her. I knew that there was really only one Penny, but I never knew she moved from Parkview to Nier. Now she's my best friend's fiancée?

'How strange and unexpected.'

I really should call more often. It has seemed as though *everything* has changed. Everything and everyone. I've changed, Wes has changed, John has changed, Justin might have changed, Mrs. Adams has changed, and Kirsten has changed. Is there anyone who still remains the same as before? Probably not. Bobo? Probably not.

"You should get some rest; we both should. We've learned so much in such a little time. I'll make sure to call you...soon, Al." She said softly. "Go get some rest, don't think so much about your next move with the boys, but just don't be stupid."

"Goodnight, Kirsten."

"Love you, Kitty cat." She said. I could feel her smile through the phone.

"Love you too, Kirs-cross."

We hung up and I placed the phone on my nightstand. So, I went out to go and take Bobo so that Wes could go and get the beds into my room. Mom and John where in the kitchen, table holding hands across the table. There was a glass of orange juice on the table. It reminded me of something lonely. There was only one glass of orange juice on the table. It was a little loner. I walked over to the living room. Bobo crawled his little body to me and I picked him up.

"Go, Wes." I told him.

Wes stood up from the couch and head upstairs.

"Al!" John called.

I walked over to the kitchen and looked at them looking at us.

"I'm so sorry, Sweetie." Seashell said. "I didn't realize what," she hiccupped. "I was doing."

"I have nothing to say." John said.

"Not like I want to hear it either." I told him.

"Al, please. I really am sorry. I didn't think about anything. I wasn't thinking; I was drunk! Forgive me. Don't leave. John will leave!" She pleaded.

John's face was priceless. It was as if something had terrified him, something big.

"No, mom. Let John stay, I'll take Wes and Bobo and move to the Wichita Mountains. You two will stay here. I will no longer take care of you, mom, John will. Nothing that happens between you two will mean anything to me. I won't care. You will not contact me or call for any reason at all. If you die, that's on the other's shoulders. You will stay with mom and if you can't handle it take her somewhere, but not to me. I am finished."

At that moment, something happened. Mom understood. She'd realize that because of how things became so messed up, she lost three things in her life. She's lost us. John could go and suck something for all I care. Now, Wesley, Bobo are my number one priority. I will continue to raise them and I will be there for them.

When it was time for bed, I went upstairs and Wes was lying on his mattress on the floor looking up at the ceiling. I changed Bobo's dipper and went back downstairs for his bottle. I placed him in his crib and he'll fall asleep sooner or later. I laid on my bed and joined Wesley at looking at my ceiling.

"What's going to happen now?" He asked.

"...We're leaving. When The Store gives me my check plus the bonus I will go down to the Wichita Mountains and find a different job. You and Bobo will come live with me. We can visit Seashell and you can have your own mountain bike. You will get a job and help me raise Bobo. We are all we have left, Wes."

It took a minute until he said, "Okay. I will."

Apparently, life comes filled with difficulties and dramas and extremely unexpected and suspenseful parts, but you just have to take it. It will make you strong. I've lived with my mother for nine years, taking care of her, Wesley, and Bobo. John did shit. So, John really wanted to take Bobo and mom off somewhere. I had a hunch. Mom, I think, was lead to getting drunk and was pressured into doing this. John knew she would, I knew she would. After dad's death everything changed. Mom truly lost her mind and I really did grow up. I became that person, that one special person, for three souls. Though, I wasn't always there to be the Wes's protector, and apparently, it's okay to have him taking care of me sometimes. Bobo will grow up with us. He loves animals and loves the outdoors; at least he loves our backyard.

My job at The Store was lots of help for getting us this far. We now live in the Wichita Mountains and we all have our own rooms. Justin..., he said that when he graduates he will come live with us. I will graduate here and so will Wesley and hopefully Bobo. The house has two floors and it's gorgeous. The boys helped pick out the decorations. There is nothing we brought from Phlox.

Three years later, and we're one big happy family. Justin is my husband, Wesley is my brother, and Bobo is still with us. He said that it'd be nice to know his father, but he wouldn't trade us for some guy who never had the guts to go and take care of him. I still hold possession of daddy's car. It's mine until the day I die. So, I don't go visiting dad every Friday anymore, but I do. Sometimes we all go and drive up to Phlox to visit him. I have the feeling that he likes the outcomes of things. Wes and I still go and bring him Irises from The Store. I visit Ariadne. We're close friends now. Kirsten and I fell a little distant, but we're still friends. Strange, how I'm actually *friends* with Aria. Anyhow, life here is good. It's quiet and serene and peaceful. It's how I'd imagined it. Bobo does go out with Wesley on their mountain bikes and they go for a ride. I stay home and clean sometimes. I like it, it's peaceful. Reminds me of the moments I'd had, the peaceful moments I'd love so much back at Phlox. We've moved on and we're together. So, maybe now everything isn't as unexpected as I thought. Maybe one day things *will* go back to how they were.

Maybe dad's looking down on us *and* taking care of mom. However it is that things are now, I wouldn't trade it for the world. Wesley and I will always be together, it couldn't be any other way. We've made it this far and we might as well get through the rest of it together as well.

Something Unexpected 2

I waited quietly in the living room, waiting for Justin and Wesley to come back from the store a few miles away. I swear, I waited and waited but it seemed as though time was moving faster and faster and everything else around me just stopped and froze, while time moved and kept going and going and going. The test was positive, my heart was racing, and I was going crazy. How could I have possibly come out with this conclusion? How could this have happened? I wanted things to calm down, I wanted me to calm down and for the boys to come back. Bobo was out on the mountain bike and I really didn't need him to come back. At this point, I couldn't care less whether Bobo returned or not. Bobo just left and didn't even ask me if I needed anything from him before he left! How would he know if I were to need something from him? He wouldn't, because he didn't ask. What if I needed a burger and there was *no more food* and I hadn't eaten for days? He wouldn't have known, because he didn't ask, because he was too concerned with his mountain bike that he couldn't have found enough time in the clock to ask if I needed a simple, stupid, burger!

My stomach curled inside of me and my breath became bitter and disgusting to bear. Throw up. I ran to the bathroom as fast as my legs could go. It was a close call but I managed to make it to the sink just in time. It was disgusting and my breath smelled completely revolting. After it was gone I brushed my teeth and tried to calm down in the sofa. I turned on the TV. It was strange to think that I was throwing up and there was no one here with me to ask me what was going on. It felt...different. I was used to being alone. Justin went to work far, far from here. Bobo usually went from home to school to some friend's home to coming back home. Wesley works at some gasoline station not that far from here but still far. So, I'm usually at home, cleaning, cooking, like I thought I would be. It's nice to know that I was right, but now I'm afraid that I won't be doing anything else. It was nice to think that life would be calm and simple, but not this calm and simple. The television is a hated item in my house now and it irritates me even more now that I have nothing to do but watch it, makes me feel as though it won a battle between us. As if I lost and it won, I will watch it to keep from being bored. But then I thought,

'It doesn't have to end like this. I won't loose to a stupid computer with moving pictures.'

I got up from the sofa, turned off the TV, and walked over to the kitchen. I began to make some soup. I still remember back when Wes made me that soup,   because he thought it would make me feel better, because in theory that is what we believed healed a person.

Minutes after I had finished washing the dishes the boys came in through the door. Bobo was the first to come through. He came in with a girl, who was wrapped against his chest, like she was hugging him.

"Al, this is..., uh. What's your name?" He asked her.

"Gloria; like the kid from Viva la Gloria, the song from Green Day. My folks are big fans. They once went to one of their concerts and ended up at the back of a delivery truck with about five dozen-"

"Okay, let's go, Gloria. Call when foods ready?"

"...Sure." I answered.

Wesley and Justin came in, laughing, when Bobo and his friend went pass the kitchen to his room outside. He didn't wanted to be under the same roof as us so we told him that he can take the barn. It's good enough, I guess.

"We got food that could last a lifetime." Wes said.

"Yeah, depending on how much you'll eat a day." Justin joked with Wes.

At this point both of them were carrying tons of plastic bags with food inside. I was as still as a stone. When they had finished carrying all of the groceries from the car to the kitchen Wes went up to the bathroom, I think. I wasn't thinking very well, my heart began to pound. It was going really fast and most of my sentences in my head won't form right. It was as if I was paralyzed and had suddenly become stupider. Justin walked up to me; I was standing between the living room and the kitchen, and he took my hands in his.

"Owlina." He said it as he looked like he was chewing a gun. "Owlina." He said when I wouldn't answer.

He took my shoulders and shook me well enough that my insides would probably have become jelly thanks to him. That did the complete opposite of helping. I was going to barf again. I could smell it coming like some unwelcomed creature. I knew that this time I wouldn't make it pass the kitchen and into the bathroom so I just went straight for the sink in the kitchen. It was still as disgusting as the first time. When I had finished brushing my teeth again in the bathroom sink, Justin looked at me. He didn't come over to me and I think it was because he thought I was going to throw up again.

"Did I do that? Al, I'm really sorry. I shouldn't have. Are you okay, did I hurt you? Are you going to throw up again? Should I get you anything?"

There we go! The one question I wanted someone to ask me. Not even my own brothers asked me. I had to wait until my husband and brother got back from grocery shopping to have been asked one *stupid* question!

"No, you didn't do anything. I'm...not feeling well." I think I said that in a kind of sarcastic, trying to be funny without wanting to be funny, kind of way. "But, I'll just try to rest it off."

"Do you want me to make you something?"

"I just had soup."

When I saw that his whole body relaxed, even if it did just a little bit, I walked up to him and wrapped my arms around him. He laid his head on mine and I could feel something, something that's not usually there. I had *no* idea what it is, but it *was* there. I couldn't stop hugging him, because whatever it was, it was stopping me from wanting to release my grip from him. I didn't want to anyway. I stay home alone more than what I wish I did and having my husband here really makes me happy.

"You okay?" He asked without moving his head from above mine.

"..." I hummed him my answer and he agreed.

"What?"

"We should do something. We agreed that you are *not* okay." He looked down at me then.

"Yes, I am." I said.

"No, you aren't." Then he remembered. "Well, you have to rest or something. Throwing up is not right. We can take you to the hospital if you need me to, love."

There goes that holy word I love to hear... **Need**. Need is something very strong and powerful to me. I need this, I need that. I need my family, the one I wanted since before Bobo was born.

"I'll like that. No wait! No. I do not necessarily want access to have you take me to the hospital." I took a step away as I let go of him. I tried not to use the word need, but I don't think I need a very good job.

"So..., no hospital?" He seemed more than confused, it was adorable.

"No." I answered with a laugh.

"Okay." He shook his head.

"..." There were no words left to say.

Suddenly, out of the blue, I get this pulse that urges me to just...go. I rush my way back to Justin and take *his face* in *my hands* and I start making out with him like if it was the end of the world. It was crazy, I know. I love to kiss my husband, but it was crazy how it just felt like an "I have to" more than an "I want to." I truly do love to kiss him, but why did this time it just felt really different. I kissed him for about a whole minute until I stopped to get air. His eyes were fixed on my eyes and down to my lips and back to my eyes and so on.

"Al! What's going on?" He asked as his face was still clutched in my hands.

"I have no idea, but I think I like it." I told him.

I went back in for seconds. This time it was only a matter of seconds before he pulled away from my face. He held on to my hands on his face and soon enough he took my hands off his face and lowered them down, but still in his hands.

"This is not like you, Owlina." He tried to sound firm. "Tell me what's going on? I want to know, so if there is I can help you. What's going on?" He asked. "What's happening to my little flower?" He asked more softly but still as romantic.

"Justin, I don't know."

A minute later I said, "Do you like it here?"

"..." He looked at me...puzzled. Like if my question was part of some surprise trivia. "What kind of question is that? Of course I like it here? Don't you? It's that it? Do you want to move?" He held me closer. "We'll move if you want to."

"...I don't...want to move."

"Then, why the question?"

"I meant, do you like it here, just being the four of us; you, me, Wes, and Bobo? Is it enough people for you to be living with or...no?"

"...Al, you're loosing me."

I took a second to think about what I was going to say next. Then I took back one of my hands and led the way to the sofa. He sat down and I sat on his lap as he wrapped his arms around me like some big and warm blanket.

"Okay." He whispered.

"...I've been thinking."

"Oh, no."

"Calm down, you haven't heard me yet. I was thinking, if you don't like the number of people here...we can change it." I wondered if my hints were of any help to him.

"You mean like...kick one of us out? Is it me? Do you want to get rid of me that quickly?"

"Don't joke. I'm trying to be serious...and quickly? It's been years, hon." And I was, but he just wasn't making things any easier or better by making jokes.

"Sorry, continue."

"Baby..., my love..., the light of my soul..., the peanut to my butter..., the bottom feeder of my aquarium, I love you. I don't know how to come out with this, but how would you feel if it wasn't just Bobo and Wesley and you and me? What if...we were more?" I hope he gets it now.

"As in..., kids?" He seemed extremely shocked. Like if it was impossible for me to *ever* get pregnant with *his* kid. I laughed a little but I was pretty mad.

"Yes."

"...Are you... pregnant, Owlina?" He moved so that he could see my face now.

My entire face went warm; I was probably red all over. I didn't know how we to got to this conclusion, how to *tell* him and how to stop with the little baby hints. Inside I felt a little glow, but it didn't come from me, it was a little bit of light, love, maybe something that I could feel as warmth, coming from Justin. My right arm was laying on his chest and stomach...and that's where it was coming from.

"You're happy." I said softly.

"I'm surprised most of all."

"But you're happy." My face grew a smile...and excitement.

"...You are pregnant." He came with the conclusion.

"..." I stood forward and then stood up on the floor. "I, Owlina Misty Parker, am pregnant with Justin Robert Van Berg's son or daughter and I," I lowered my loud voice, "Could not be any happier." I sat next to him on the sofa this time.

His face was normal and it didn't show anything different, as if I had not just confessed that I was *pregnant* with his *kid*...or kids.

"I took the test more than less than a month ago, it's been a few weeks...of...throw up. When you were all gone one day I took the car and headed done to a gas station and took the test there. I took three different ones and they all said I was pregnant."

"..."

"Say something." I said a bit cheerfully.

"...I am not leaving you alone. I'm taking some time off my job to help you. You probably do need me and you should have told me sooner." The holy word. "I will get you anything and everything. This baby will have things and nice ones and don't think that we won't-"

"I want to start working after this devil child is born."

"...Devil child?"

"...I don't know! Maybe, maybe not, whatever! I am going to start working and want to go to work when he's out!" I began to yell like if something wrong had just happened.

"Oh, I see...mood swings. Well, you can't and won't, the baby will need you to keep it healthy by feeding him and well really, just by being his...mom." I felt that little tingle of happiness again.

"...Fine, once that's taken care of I'll go to work." I said cheerfully.

"...Okay then, settled."

So that was that, I would finish raising the kid and then I could go to work.

When Justin had finished cooking he made me get out of bed and come downstairs so that all of us could eat together, including...Gloria. Wes helped Justin   prepare the table while Bobo brought the food over. Usually all of this is my job. Again, it feels different to have someone else doing my job for me.

The dining table was a present from Aunt Karen, thanking us for all of our hard work with mom. The china cups and plates were a gift from her as well. This one was a welcome present, to our new life. She promised that she would go and check on mom every now and then to make sure that everything's okay, so far so good. John found a different job. He used to work for some guys in the delivery business, the one with ships and that smelly fish smell. Yeah, well now he works at the post office back in Phlox. Mom says she's good enough to work, but I don't think so. She's still crazy and she's still not all that well. Even if it's been years since daddy's death, it's understandable because he was the only one and the first one she's ever loved so much. The only one she's ever had two kids with, her *first* two kids. I don't think, thinking about it now, that it was necessary for me to have been so hard-

"Shall we pray?" Justin asked when everyone was down in a seat.

The phloxes in the crystal vase where dead in the middle of the table, while they were begging huddled around by the food; it felt like home. Justin, Wesley, Bobo, and his guest. We were all here...with extra.

"We pray?" Bobo asked.

"Oh, can I do it? I have to practice for when I go and see my father up north in a few months. He's a very important priest up there. That's the whole reason why my folks got divorced. My mom doesn't exactly believe or care or likes any of those things that have to do with the Devil, let alone God. He has this really nice wife; they got married on my birthday so they never really come to any of my parties. Even if the parties are for teens only, they should at least write that they-"

"You should pray now." Bobo whispered as he cuffed his hands.

I gave Justin the "are you nuts" look and he smiled at me. Then we all waited until Gloria cuffed her hands and lowered her head so that we could do the same. We normally don't pray, but it usually means that something has to change when we do decide to pray. This time it was Justin's idea to pray, probably for me.

"That was...something." Wes said when she was done.

"Be nice, Wes." I said as I took the bowl of mashed potatoes.

"That was lovely, Gloria. We're glad to have you." Justin told her.

"Thanks, I'm glad to be here. You know, mom doesn't really cook." She took the pot of Mac and Cheese and began to pour some into her plate. "She gives me money to go and buy Burger King or McDonald's burgers. After a while she got really fat-"

"Eat…, its good." Bobo said without a drop of food on his plate.

"Wes…, how's work?" I asked.

"Oh, you'll love this. The other day this woman comes in with her convertible parked right where it shouldn't have. She's about five-two and with twisted orange hair. She goes and gets three chips and two bottles of water and walks over to the cash register. Brook tells her that that's fifteen dollars and the woman starts to *freak out*. She took like about seven candies from the shelf and she threw them everywhere. When she was finished with her mess she looks at Brook and tells her that that's fifteen bucks. Brook and I start *laughing* and the lady starts to get even more irritated." Wesley began to laugh again. "So she drops everything she has on the floor and she's planning on leaving. So when she goes outside, me and Brook follow her… The tow truck had just left the station and…you see the lady jumping up and down in anger. At this point it was a miracle that neither of us had peed our pants. The lady comes over to us and asks why they are taking her car. We tell her that that was fifteen dollars and she gets even more upset. Now the lady was as red as her hair and me and Brook couldn't hold it anymore. I looked over to Brook and she was about to go and run inside. I ask her what happened and she said that her pee came out."

All of us were already laughing with him, but now all of us burst in extreme laughter with Wes.

"The lady stops and looks at us weird. She starts giggling and I tell her to come inside so she could pay for her mess. She looks at me and says okay. Now it was just me and her and the cash register. Then she looks inside of her purse and finds out that she only has a twenty. It was a wreck so that twenty wouldn't hold it. I tell her that she can work it off and she screams at me. She said that it was my fault that the place was a mess, that they took her car, that Brook had peed her pants. Sooner or later we stopped to go and check on Brook. The lady asked her if she needed anything and Brook said...'pants.' The lady goes and takes off her pants, because she also was wearing a long enough dress. When Brook opens the door the lady gave Brook the pants and Brook put them on. Then the lady tells Brook that she needs to use the bathroom. So, Brook and I go back to the mess and try to clean up and save as many things as we can. Suddenly, we hear the lady crying and screaming from the bathroom. When we got there we told her to open the door and she did." He stopped to breathe and started to laugh. "The woman's leg was caught in the bathroom toilet. Then Brook walks away in laughter, and I'm trying not to pee my pants. The lady's just there with tears all over her face. By the time we stopped laughing the lady had practically forced her leg out. Her whole leg, from her knee down   was covered in water. She comes out of the bathroom looking like a hot mess and tells me, 'I think I'll take that, boy.'"

We all laughed together at Wesley's story.

"That was some...day, Wes." Justin said in-between laughs.

"The funny part of it all is that the lady had to go and walk all the way up to Frère County to go pick up her car. She called us and told us that she couldn't take it because the people that had towed her car left it outside and some raccoons took position of it. A skunk or two show up there every now and then."

At the end of the dinner Gloria offered to clean up. She said that she had to practice to be a good housewife, in case her father decides to match her up with someone better than Bobo when she goes to visit him. I took the time to watch some of the maternal TV shows in my room while Wes...did something and Justin...did something else. I felt really relaxed and comfortable in my bed. Justin wanted a big bed; he said that he never had a big bed before and that now that we both get to share a bed we can get a really big one. In the shows that I saw there were ladies from the 70s talking about being a mother and their own ways of getting ready for a baby. Other shows just showed the getting-ready part of a mother-to-be's life and her giving birth to her baby or babies. In time I got bored and watched different things. Wesley knocked the door as he was walking in with caution.

"Come in." I told him.

He shut the door behind him and laid down on the bed with me, technically he jumped right onto the bed.

"What's going on, sis?" He asked.

"Nothing, just here watching TV."

He turned his attention to the television and asked why I was watching some kid show. I hadn't realized that I was.

"Oh..., I don't know." I turned off the TV. "What have you been up to?"

"Not much. Talking to some friends from back at Phlox, they still got my number from when I first called them all."

"That's nice. I haven't talked to Aria in forever. She stopped calling and answering my calls all at once."

"What about... What's her name? Uh..., Maple? No..., Autumn? No..., uh. **KIRSTEN**!"

"What about her? We fell apart years ago."

"Oh..., that's sad. So, how are things?"

Me not talking to Kirsten has not made any difference in my life. I lost Kirsten, but gained Ariadne. She and I have really gotten close ever since the whole apology thing at my house that one night.

"How do you feel about being an uncle, Wes?" I asked.

"Are you kidding? If either of you comes to me with a little niece or nephew I will take that kid and never give him back to you. I will love that little son or daughter of a gun. Why the question?"

"..." I smiled. "I'm pregnant, Wes."

His face went really...bright. Like a little glow of happiness Wesley got a smile on his face. It got bigger and bigger as the seconds passed. Then he sat up and gave me a gigantic hug as he was kissing my cheeks.

"I take it your happy." I said as soon as I could breathe.

"Are you joking?" He released me and sat up straight. "You're making me an uncle; I will love you forever for this, kid. But I must warn you, I will want to spoil him or her." He said.

"Are you sure about that?"

"Positive. I want to give her everything!"

We laughed and talked about the kind of goofed up dad Justin might be. After a while he kissed me one last time and left the room. I heard shouting and laughter not long after. Justin must have been screaming with Wes. That's one thing about Wes that I like. Wes doesn't care who's around or who looks, he will act the way he wants to when he wants to.

Maybe this whole pregnancy thing won't be all that hard. Maybe the ladies on TV just make it look more difficult than what it really is for television sake. I suppose that had to be true. That *my* pregnancy will go smoothly and that our baby will come out safe and sound and healthy as either one of. Maybe life isn't all that hard when you look at it from the pregnant lady's point of view. My point of-

I got out of bed as soon as possible and head to the bathroom in our room. The sink was there, welcoming me to throw up in it. Telling me that it was okay to throw up, because somehow it was good for little baby Edward. The throw up, I wondered if this was going to be an hourly thing.

"Al?" Justin's calming voice said as he came into the room.

I pounded on the sink to let him know where I was.

"Oh, ew." He laughed as his reaction. "I heard the tumbling of your feet running so I came up to see what's going on. Me and my noisy self. I'll be back in a few minutes to make sure you're okay. Do you want to eat anything else? Soup, corn...? You know how much you love your corn."

"...N..., No thanks. I'm super tired anyways, so I'll just go to bed. Check in later, okay?"

"Of course." He said.

He walked up to me and kissed the top of my head and slowly walked out as he left the door opened, when he knows I hate doors being left opened.

I wouldn't mid throwing up all this much if I was sure that it was good for the baby. I was just a little scared because in the process of throwing up I can't exactly breathe very well, so it does scare me a little that it might affect the baby even in the smallest way.

Now it was the bed that welcomed me. Its tongue was getting ready to accept me and to hold me for my rest. I slipped in with my slippers and placed the blanket over me. I slipped slowly away from reality, knowing that I was never welcome back to Short Rainbows...I didn't even try to go back. Instead, months ago, I came upon a new world. One filled with things and people I like. My good friend, Lollipop Lucy, left her life back in Short Rainbows to come with me. She and I came across each together by accident one night, and since then we've done everything together, like little girls or teenage girls do. It seems childish now that I think about it, but the only *true* friend that I really *do* have...isn't real. It seems pathetic to me. All grown up and still without a girl to call my friend, my best friend. The first person that would come to mind would be Kirsten, but...yeah. So, next it was... Aria. Ariadne is a really sweet girl, maybe even sweet enough that I'll see her in Willow Meadow. Mom was there...and dad. John better never show his face around here. Wesley, of course, and Justin are here. For some reason I can't seem to be able to bring in Bobo, I think that that means something.

In the morning, when I woke up, I felt normal. The first thing that came to mind was why was I throwing up so much? I haven't even been more than a month pregnant, is this normal? I wouldn't know. The TV shows don't really give all of that information, and I could go to a library, but I'd be lucky if I could find a hippy who knows about pregnancy. Actually, I could probably just find a hippy; it's more likely that I'll find him instead of a library. I love libraries. They're filled with stories and poems and they smell so good. Now I want to go to a library.

"Hey, Al." Wes greets me when I get to the living room.

"... Hey."

I'm looking around and it's really quiet. There isn't a Bobo in sight or a Justin either. It reminds me of the library. I love Green Eggs and Ham! It was the first book I read when I was able to read. Maybe I can get it and read it to Jason. I love Miss Rumphius, too.

"Where's everyone?" I asked.

"Justin is working. Bobo is-"

"It's Saturday!" I protest.

Wesley gets up from laying down and relaxing on the couch and comes to me. He holds on to my shoulders and tells me, "He's working."

It's Saturday! I'm pregnant! I want my husband! I can't believe he would do such as thing! He himself told me that he is not leaving me alone. That he is taking some time off his job to help me. That "you probably do need me and you should have told me sooner. I will get you anything and everything. This baby will have things and nice ones and don't think that we won't-" Then I remember I interrupted him. But he said it himself and now he should keep his word.

"I know he should, if he said that." Wes says.

"...What?" I asked in shock and complete terror.

"That if Justin really said all of that than he should keep his word. He should be here with you." Wes said.

"...But I... I didn't say that."

"...Yes, you did. I heard it as clear as how you're talking right now."

"Wesley..., I'm really sure that I... **I would have noticed**. It's not like me to say things and then think that I *didn't*!"

"...You hungry?" He asked.

"...Starving."

"*Good*. Cuz', someone's little brother can cook and bake and bring you up some wonderful pancakes." He offered.

"..."

"Unless you have baby-cravings now." He said more normally.

"...Well, if it's the baby or not I'm sure I don't want pancakes."

We should go out instead. I want some fresh air and food.

"...How about I make us some bacon and scrambled eggs and toast, and then we can go and eat it outside instead. Deal?"

'Freaky.'

"Sure."

"Alright." He laughed. "Go get ready and I'll get it done."

I nodded my head and then walked myself upstairs. When I came back downstairs I felt less than normal, I felt pregnant, less than a month of this and I feel more pregnant than ever. How is this possible? Just a while ago I felt normal. Not that   there's anything wrong with feeling pregnant, since I am and I'm not planning on hiding it, but it doesn't feel like me. I feel fat. Like if I gained about five or seven pounds in the pass weeks. Nothing right now could make me feel any better. This was an all time low.

"Come on now." Wes rushed calmly as he saw me taking my time, making my way to the kitchen table.

"I'll be there when I'm there." I told him.

"...Al." He looked at me as if I was twenty times bigger than normal and blue. He looked at me as if I was something he didn't know.

"What?" I asked harshly.

"Are you...okay?"

"... Of course not!" I could feel my walk; how I was walking. I was walking like those pregnant women I love to make fun of so much. "Look at me, Wesley! I'm huge!"

"...I honestly don't think there's any difference." He answered a bit loudly.

"I grew like seven pounds in about an hour!" I barked.

"Maybe you're just making room for the baby." Uncle Wes thought.

"I don't want to make too much room, Wesley!" I began to cry. "I don't want to be fat, Wes."

"Aw, come on, Al. Even a few extra pounds are good now and then...for anyone. When my little niece is out, don't worry, we'll take you to the gym or buy you things to go and loose those little leftovers. Okay?" He said as he robbed my shoulders.

"..." I didn't have words.

In my mind I wanted to answer him in some way but, I don't know, I just didn't. I was just too busy thinking about the baby and my *fat* body that answering him wasn't really quite important at the time.

"Okay, okay. Let's go. You little missy, wipe those tears and I'll serve you a plate. Go outside, I'll be right there."

I nodded my head and slowly walked to the backyard. It's pretty nice. I see mountains far away. We have grass here and then there's a fence. I hate those kinds of fences that typical Americans have; the white fences. They are really not original and too dull for my style. Our fence is just a fence; it's not made out of wood.

"Okay, now. I want to see a smile. Who's the best brother *you*'ve ever had?" He asks as he walks out with a plate in each hand.

"...You are." I say, almost as a question.

"... Aw." He stops in his tracks.

"...You're the best brother I have *ever* had! Do you even know how *lucky* I am to even have you?" I tried my best.

He gets a gigantic smile on his face and keeps walking to me on the bench. After bringing out the orange juices he sat and we started eating.

"Good?" He asks after a little while.

"Yup," I tried to keep it short.

"How's life as a going-to-be-mother?" He asks.

I stare up at him in a bit of shock, my face remained the same.

"...I feel fat, and hungry, and I need my husband!" I protested. "Is this how it's going to be when I'm *months* old... or worst?"

I feared it. I was not just worried about me physically, but me...and the baby. If I eat too much, will this mean that the baby will end up being fat?! No! I don't want a *fat* baby, or a fat kid. Though..., fat babies do look pretty cute and there is much more room for hugs and cuddles if you have a bigger body.

"...I'll call him right away." Wes took his empty plate and cup and went inside.

Since Phlox we upgraded. We got cell phones, well, at least Justin got his...and Wes has his...and Bobo has his..., I get the house phone. I don't really like not having my own cell phone, but I don't really mind it. I mean, who will I talk to of I had it; no one, certainly not my best friend. Why would Lollipop Lucy want to talk to me in the real world when I see her most of the time anyways.

After I had finished, I went and brought my things inside. I washed them and left them alone to dry. I took sometime to myself and relaxed on the couch. Laying down on this couch makes everything worth it.

I closed my eyes and pictured myself in Rome. I always wanted to go to Rome; it looked amazing from the TV screen.

"I called Justin." Wesley told me a little later.

"...Where is he?" I asked as I opened my eyes; to find him standing next to me.

"He's...in Phlox."

The hell is he doing way up in Phlox? He's suppose to be *here*...with me and little Jackson. I just gained a whole new perspective towards him.

"...Why?" I asked.

"...He's doing something."

He's not telling me everything. Why? Why would Wes not tell me something as important as this? What's going on?!

"What's going-"

"I don't know. I...well, I *do* know, but I can't let *you* know. Not just yet. I'll make it up to you, but just don't ask questions. Please, don't get mad. What do you want? I'll go and bring it to you." He said.

"...I want my husband!" I began to cry.

"He'll be here. He'll need sometime to get back, but he'll be here."

"...Why didn't he tell me?" I asked in-between breaths.

"...It's...not coming out of *my* mouth." He told me. "But he'll be here. So, just give it time. In the mean while, do you want to go somewhere?"

Where my husband is at!

"Al," Wes said...almost beggingly.

"...I want ice-cream."

"...Okay, let me go and get my keys and we'll go."

I waited until he left to go and get my shoes. I wore my normal flip-flops and went downstairs to the driveway. He was pulling out the truck, his truck. I went back to go and locked the doors, and then I went and got inside of the car once he's closed the garage door.

"How long?" I asked after about a minute of driving.

"A few miles, calm down."

He did something that made me smile then. He turned on the radio and put on the station that we both love so much. Our dear **MCR** was playing *Sing*.

"I love them." Wes said as he turned it up, like old times, except that this time Wes was the one driving.

"...Sing it for the boys. Sing it for the girls. Every time that you loose it sing it for the world." I sang-along.

"Sing it from the heart!" Wesley yelled.

"Sing it till you're nuts."

"Sing it out for the one that'll hate your guts!"

So, we sang the rest of the time there. Some songs we didn't know so we just played a short game of "I spy" and then kept on singing if we knew a song.

"Good morning. Welcome to Daily Freeze, go ahead and order whatever you want when you're ready." The lady inside told us.

"...I want a small chocolate ice-cream. That's it for me." Wesley told her.

"I want a medium vanilla milkshake with no whip cream and I still want the cherry." I told her.

"...It might sink-"

"I know."

"...That'll be three dollars."

Wesley took out three dollars from his wallet in his back pocket and paid the lady. After getting our ice-cream and milkshake I headed back to the car. Wesley stayed behind a little while longer.

"What's that all about?" I asked him when he came back.

"...What?"

"Why did you stay back? Do you like her?" I asked then I took a sip out of the straw.

"...She's okay. But really I wanted to ask her what was going on with Brook."

"...From the station?"

"Yeah. She hasn't showed up in about a week and I got worried."

"... What would she know about Brook?" I asked.

He laughed, "That's her sister, Al."

'Stupid.'

"Oh, sorry." I took another sip. "Did you get anything?"

"...Brook's in the hospital." He said sadly.

"...Wes..., I'm so-"

"Don't say it, it's not you're fault." He licked his ice-cream. "Brook has this thing," he began to wiggle his fingers in front of his stomach. "In her stomach that can be 'painful' and they're looking for ways on how to get it out of her."

"...It?" I got worried.

"It's a parasite. It's living inside of one of her organs and they're looking for ways on how to get it out without hurting her." He tried to sound hopeful.

"...Are you going to go visit her?"

"...Yeah, I'll go. Daisy gave me the number of her room and told me when I can go visit her."

"Well then good!" I said. "You'll go visit her and you'll be happy."

"...I guess."

We were silent for a while, until I turned on the radio.

Wes took our time going home. He said that he didn't wanted me to be trapped inside of the house for all of this time, so he drove us to some friend's house.

"Who lives here?" I asked.

"...You'll see." He smiled as he got ready to leave the car.

Though it hasn't been more than a month, I could feel pregnant even if I didn't seem to be all that much. So, getting out of the car wasn't as easy as always, I wonder why. I mean really it's just a baby not some military *tank* inside of me. Wasn't it?

Wesley knocked the door three times and a very adorable old man came to the door. He was a bit taller than Justin and he was blond. Speaking of blonds, Bobo really is a blond. He's as blond as Farrah Fawcett now.

"Hello?" The man said.
"Hi there, is Luke home?" Wesley asked him.
"Well, yes he is."

The man opened the screen door and we passed him by. He led us to the living room and we sat on the chairs by the table.

"And you must be..." He said.
"Uh, sorry. I'm Wesley and this is my sitter, Al, and my niece, Rebecca." Wesley robbed my belly.
"Or nephew, Jensen." I said.
The man laughed. I like Rebecca.

"I'll go get Luke out for you."
"Who's Luke?" I asked when the man was gone.
"A friend."
"Do I *know* him?"
"I don't think so." Wes said.

A lady came out with a silver tray of biscuits and cookies and all sorts of good treats.

'Delicious.'

"Hello, Wesley." She said.
"Good morning, Mrs. John." Wes said.

"Hello, dear. Treat?" She told me.

"Oh, thank you." I said.

She put down the food on the table and I began to eat everything in sight.

"Al!" Wes said.

"Ha-ha. It's quite alright, dear. I remember when I was pregnant with Luke, the poor thing always made me hungry!" She laughed. "He was always kicking; always kicking." She repeated. "The little thing was *huge* by the time he came out!"

Huge! As in...really big and fat?! As in...wouldn't it hurt even more!? My baby always makes me eat a lot and it's not even a month. What if my baby comes out huge!? What if I die because of it?

"Okay! That's enough, Mrs. John." Wesley said.

"Oh, well. Alright." She walked her little wrinkled self away.

It wasn't long until another person came into the room. He greeted Wesley and shook my hand. Then he went and sat on one of the chairs from the table.

"So, this is the famous Al I've heard almost too much about?" Luke looked at Wesley and then at me.

"Yup, that's her. My big sister." Wes said.

"And it's true that you're going to be mom?"

"Yeah." I answered in-between bites.

Wesley and Luke laughed.

After our little time of having fun and eating other people's food, we left around four. It was a pretty nice day, then it happened. About two miles from home,

"Stop the car!" I told Wesley.

He didn't even bother to ask why. He just stopped the car right there and I ran out of it. I threw up about six feet away from the car. It was pretty big and it took a lot longer that usual. I figured it was just the food that the lady gave me. Maybe it must have upset my stomach and the baby. Will he be a kid that doesn't like sugar? I hope so, sugar is good but it can give really bad stomach pains. Why would I want my baby to go through those?

"All better?" Wes asked when I got back.

"I think. Just hurry." I told him.

At home I threw up once more, right when I got in. I didn't have time to get to any sink. The foyer smelled horrible. Wesley told me to go and get some ginger ale and he'll clean up the mess.

"Thanks." I told.

"Of course." He said.

When I had finished a whole bottle of it I went to go and relax in my bed. I was thinking about Justin and what he must have been doing back in Phlox. Is he cheating on me? Because I'm going to be fat and I 'm going to throw up a lot more he's going to go and find some chick to cheat on me with. That got me thinking. We have to go back and v i s i t daddy some time. I wonder if he knows that I'm pregnant. If he knows then would I feel better, somehow? Wouldn't I be happier, even a little bit? I feel terrible! I want my husband! I want to go see daddy! I'm exhausted.

I gave up my strength to keep arguing about things I'm mad about and went to sleep. Apparently, I had slept the entire rest of that day. About seven days later, in the morning, I found Justin sleeping next to me in bed. How un**expected**!

I began to hit him and I started to feel better. I took my anger and frustrations out on him not being with me. I woke him up.

"Hey. Hey. **Hey**!" He said.

He grabbed my hands and then kissed my cheek.

"Baby, I'm sorry."

"And to *whom* are you talking to?" I asked.

He let me go.

"Where were you!? Well, I *know* where you were. You were out looking for some hoe to *please* you since I won't be able to!" I barked.

I stood up from the bed and found myself being a bit bigger than yesterday. I wobbled myself out of there and into the bathroom downstairs; the one next pass the kitchen. Justin was knocking the door, asking to let him in or to come out.

"Go away!" I cried from inside of the tub.

"No, please. What would I have to do to be forgiven? Al, please, I am so sorry."

"If...you were really sorry you wouldn't have done that!" I yelled.

I then screamed. It made me feel a little better. I was yelling at him and at the world for...everything..., global warming even.

I heard silence after a while. I must have been drunk because a light voice was coming from the door. It wasn't Justin's or Wesley's. It wasn't Bobo's or his friend's voice. It was female though. It was talking to Justin, I think.

"Al?" It called for me.

In that instead I ran to out of the tub and I opened the door. There she was. The person I wanted to see. The person I needed to see. I wrapped my arms around her and she hugged me. I could see Justin out of the corner of my eye.

"I missed you." I told her.

"I know." She told me.

"It was supposed to be a surprise." Justin said when we finished.

"You should have told me where you were. I was worried and scared and I couldn't stop throwing up." I kept crying.

Ariadne robbed my back in comfort.

"Please, I just knew you'd want to have her here so I just went to go get her." He said.

"Are you staying until he comes out?" I turned and asked her.

"Until the baby comes out? Yeah, I want to see her and see if she gets anything from me. I'll be for you, Al."

"Forgive me, love." Justin began to hold my belly and recoil me back to him.

"You, sir, are cleaning this house until it shines." I told him.

"I'll clean and clean until it shines."

I smiled up at him and kissed him. I think Aria might have left the room after that.

"Okay, go clean." I said.

"Ma'am, yes, ma'am." He said.

I went back upstairs to go and brush my teeth after a while downstairs. I found that Justin was just leaving the bathroom upstairs.

"Are you cleaning?" I asked.

"Uh huh." He said.

When I went back downstairs Bobo and Wesley were eating breakfast at the kitchen table, while Ariadne was cleaning off the stove.

"Good morning." The boys said.

It almost made me want to cry. When was the last time I had seen *both* of *my brothers* at the same time? It's been a while. I almost forgot I had *two* of those little monsters.

"Hi."

"When were you planning on tell *me*?" Bobo asked as I sat next to him.

"...Whenever, but you weren't ever here." Aria served me some cereal.

"Oh, I see. And calling me wasn't good enough?"

"It's a baby, Bobo!" That sounded funny. "I wasn't just going to call you."

"Where's Justin?" Wes asked.

"Cleaning." I said.

Wesley laughed...and Aria laughed, but Bobo was lost.

"Stop that." I told Aria. "Come eat, Justin got it."

I took a shower after that. My belly really is coming in nicely. By now, if I'm correct, it's a month. I'm a month pregnant. My baby probably will be fat, since I don't think it's normal for a baby of one month to even be this big. I think that there are tons of possibilities on why my tummy is like this, but I *know* it's not anything bad.

After Justin had finished his duty, he wanted to talk to me. So, he led me to the bedroom and closed the door behind him. It was just the two of us now on the bed.

"Al...," he begins. "How are you?"

"... Pregnant! I..." I didn't know what to say-how to answer to that kind of question.

'Are *you* okay?'

"... Why did you think that I would be going off and try to find someone? Love," he started to pull me closer to him. "I'm pretty sure that I would never be wanting to look for anyone else, but you. I will *always* make an exception for you."

He kissed my forehead as we cuddled on the bed. I had nothing to say, I was just there...listening. Though, I love how out of the blue Justin can be a very nice and romantic guy...for me, it felt weird.

"Your belly's looking big." He said after a minute of silence. "Is it normal?"

"...I don't think so, but nothing in my life has ever really *been* normal. Not even my own *brother*." I joked.

"Do you want to and get it checked?" He asked.

"...No." I said softly. "It might not look normal, or the normal size at least, but I don't feel like if there's anything wrong. As far as I'm concerned, I just have to keep throwing up and the baby will be fine."

His head was on top of mine so I couldn't really see what his reaction to that was.

"I never want you to leave me..., never again, never like that!" My heart began to race.

"Excuse me for trying to do something good for my wife." He says.

It's strange because this probably is the second time in our entire marriage that he has decided to call me his wife. It really does bother me, considering that I try to be a good enough wife for him and he doesn't even thank me by simply calling me wife, at least not as much as I want him to.

I pulled myself together and try to get away from him now. He takes a little while, thinking that we're playing, to let me go. I walk my little bubbly self to the door and stop myself from leaving when I hear him talking to me.

"Where are you going?" He moves his head over to look at me.

"...Out of here."

"What did I do?"

"Do you even *want* to be married to me? Do you even *want* this kid to come out at all? Do you even **need** me to be here with you right now?"

Everything just came out. I don't know how to explain it and I don't intend to, but I felt right. Having to say what I've been thinking for days, I wanted him to get of huge piece of my mind..., the biggest one.

He stands up from the bed and only stands next to it... away from me.

"Of course I do! I love you and I will love this baby!" He said.

'...Where's the marriage part?' At this point I feel betrayed and unloved. Does he only want me for the baby? I feel unwell and very...horrible. I've loved this man for *far* too long to end up with nothing but a *huge bowl of shit* on my plate!

"...I will not and did not go to Phlox or anywhere else to find someone to replace you." It almost convinced me. "Why *can't* you just believe me? I love *you*. Owlina Misty Parker, I do love you."

"..." I began to cry. "I'm not exactly doubting your abilities to love me, but I am doubting your abilities to even need me by your side...as your wife. I need to know if you *need* me anymore! I have your *child*...! Is this why...you don't want me anymore? You don't want me... Need me anymore because I came up as being the one that will have your kid." I said softly...almost in defeat.

He honestly had his eyes watering. He took about *two* steps towards me and stopped when he saw that I tried to move back.

"Oh my God." I say in soft horror. "It's true." The tears fell down my face. "You...don't want me any... You don't need me anymore because I...am carrying your child."

I couldn't believe it. I did have a hunch and I did have my suspicion and I did have my theory and I did have my facts..., but now I had the answer, too. Me, Owlina *Misty* Parker..., I. I can't believe it. I was being used? I was being used.

"Is this what you wanted?" I took a few breaths to *try*, unsuccessfully, and gather myself. "Is this what you needed from me all along? Is our whole marriage *a lie*? Is everything you led me to believe all a lie! How can I possibly move on now! How can I possibly move on now with **you**?! I can't! I can't."

I ran out of there as soon as I saw that little flicker, that little sign that showed me that he would try to come closer to me. I ran down the hall, the hall that I picked out every little decoration for. I ran down the stairs, the stairs that I told him to make sure were carpeted. I ran passed the foyer..., the foyer. The foyer is where this baby first... Where the baby is really from is the foyer; that night, that one *stupid* night.

I ran out of...*his* property and onto the other side of the street, still running, or trying to. I then hear Wes's voice yelling from behind. He seemed to be forever and an eternity away from me. Forever and an eternity I spent with that... Aahhh!

"Owl!" He yelled.
"Owlina!?" I heard Bobo.
When I began to slow down a bit I looked back. I wasn't as nearly as far as I thought I was. Wesley was running as fast

as he could, I could see it on his face, towards me. Bobo was still at that place. He was by the doorframe looking out. Then I see him making his way to me too. I could tell that he wasn't running or even trying as hard as Wesley, but he was.

I stopped walking when I reached this one adorable green bench that the local boys made in school for their community. I could see the house, it wasn't far... Not far enough. I let myself slip out of here. I laid my head back and rested. When I heard sounds I opened my eyes. Wesley was standing next to me on my left and Bobo was sitting next to me on my right.

"Al..., *what* happened?" Wes asked when he caught his voice.

"..." I *tried*, but only little annoying noises were coming out of my mouth.

Bobo took me under his arm and we hugged.

"I heard it all." Bobo explained. "...We don't need to talk about now, do we?" He asked.

"...Tell Wesley, Bobo." I felt like a little kid that is calling them both to be good to one another.

I came out of our hug and looked at Wesley as Bobo told him what had happened.

"It was a giant *lie*." Bobo said. "He only really wanted... the kid...a kid."

"..."

Wesley doesn't have words to share or any sounds to bring out. He has...fire in his eyes, like the way he used to when he was mad at something...back when he was little. I began to giggle a little, because thinking about things like this does make me happy. Wesley laughed a little, too.

"What's so funny?" Bobo asked.

'Why is Wesley laughing?'

"Why are you laughing?" I asked Wesley.

"Okay, so when I got mad I was pretty angry, but this is different." He gets serious.

Is it just me or is this little coincidence happening way too often? Wesley knows what's in my head.

"I don't. You're saying them out loud as clear as day." Wesley stretched out his arms towards the sky.

I stood up in pure horror and amazement.

'... Psst.'

"What?" Wesley answered.

I recoiled back.

"Am I missing something?" Bobo asked.

"...Wes." I begin. "You can read my mind. You say it sounds as clear as day, but yet you're the only one that can hear them. Bobo, the poor baby, is lost while I'm over here... figuring out that you're special, Wes. This has happened *way* too many times to be a coincident anymore." I told them.

The boys both begin to look at each other, but their faces are pointed on me. Then, they get these little smiles and they begin to laugh.

"Bobo, think something." I ordered him.

There was a little silence. Later I find Wes laughing his lungs out, while *I'm* the one that's lost. I never thought that with such news like that one from before that I could have the ability to feel any better for the rest of...this month.

"This is so freaky!" Wes said. "So, I'm psych?" He's really happy now.

"...Guess so." I said.

I then realize that this amazing news wasn't as good or powerful enough to make me happy. My face goes blank and all I want to do is faint, go dead, never have to need to look at him again. I want someone to come out of nowhere and shoot me dead. I can't believe *I* came up to *that* conclusion. I feel like throwing up, this time it's not for the baby, but for me. I need to see...if throwing up will at least help me feel better. It was just coincidence that I needed to throw up for the baby as well. I then walked behind Wesley and vomited on the grass. They both convinced me to go back to that place after my vomiting. Aria was sitting on the couch in the living room, legs crossed, and I think she was waiting for us...or me.

The boys are both at my sides, keeping me steady and preventing me from fainting. Thanks a lot, Wes. He laughed. Ariadne stood up, her face so still and with no emotions, she walked up to me and wanted a hug. The boys had refused to let me go.

"..." Aria is *also* speechless.

It's strange to consider her ever being speechless. Considering that I think of her as the one person in the world that will and could speak her mind and than not feel sorry for doing it... Aria seemed like a stranger, just standing there in front of me..., wanting to *hug* me? I don't want to hug her. In my head, as far I wanted to believe a lie, it was all her fault. Justin left and because he did everything that I had to do alone I bottled up and threw them out today. For all I *truly* know, I'm just going crazy and he does need me. Justin does want me and the baby and not just the baby.

We where in the middle of the foyer and the living room, when I see Justin out of the corner of my eye coming to us...slowly as ever possibly.

"Justin?" I said extremely soft and weak.
"No." Wes told me. "Go clean up and maybe later."

Bobo helped me to go upstairs and to get to the bathroom. I washed up my mouth and wanted to dart my way downstairs, but I felt exhausted. Unfortunately, I really wanted to sleep. Is strange that I would want to sleep after all of this, while all of this is going on? Me being pregnant can't possibly be an excuse, not to me. I needed a final answer and a conclusion and I really needed to be *up*! How could all of this happen? How could I even...be-

"Al!" Bobo yelled.

I didn't dream, not this night. I had a nightmare. I was at some crazy house for crazy people; it was very dark and spooky and mysterious, mysterious in the bad way. The people there all looked the same, but they came in different sizes, like normal people. I was dangling from a pole on the ceiling after running away from something. I think I flew up there, so I was just dangling upside down on some pole in a crazy house. The things, people, all came to me and looked at me weird. They looked at me with their unevenly sized eyes and with their strangely shaped-like-the-number-eight heads.

I woke up to the feel and warmth of fire. The first thing that came to mind was that the fireplace in the living room had been lit for some reason. I heard voices coming from the other side of the door. Once I had brushed my teeth I opened the door and walked downstairs. There were most definitely voices coming from somewhere down there. The foyer was empty, but even as I made my way to the living room I could feel that the voices were coming from somewhere else. Ariadne was sitting on the couch talking to Bobo, who was standing in front of her. She was sitting next to Gloria, who was watching the TV on the other side of the couch. I walked in and couldn't see Wesley or Jus...

"Sit down, Sweetie." Aria said as she patted the seat next to her.

I walked over and hesitated to sit down next to her and Gloria, but I did.

"How's the baby?" Gloria turned to me and asked me.

"I think he's okay?" I said shyly.

"Good, great. You know, when I was a baby in my mom's stomach she told me that she drank a lot and that dad once dropped me and I hit the carpeted floor on my head. I could've dead, but I didn't, because mom was a nurse. Yeah, well, she got fired, but she was a nurse." Gloria surprisingly finished.

It's not really nice to interrupt someone, even if they're annoying. You should always have at least *some* manners.

"That's great, Gloria." I responded.

Now, I'm looking around the room; Wesley and Justin weren't in sight, yet. I would ask Aria where they've gone, but wouldn't that just make me look even more desperate than what they already think I am?

"Hey..." Aria said to me. "How are you? Are you feeling better, Sweetie?"

"Yeah, I think I'm better." I couldn't look at her; I wouldn't, so I looked down at my little bump that is my stomach.

"Justin and Wes went out." Bobo tells me after I feel him looking at me.

I raised my head as fast as possibly and looked at him... puzzled I am.

"Where are they?" I wanted to scream as I spoke, but how rude would that have seemed to Gloria?

"..." Bobo exhaled. "Al, are you hungry? I can make you something if you'd like."

"I am hungry, but I want to know where they are. And why are you guys here? What's going on!?"

I wonder why is it that so many unexpected things are happening. Why is it that Justin would decide to do this? He knows what we've been through and yet he hasn't..., or didn't have any sympathy. Then again I never did let him explain. And then again how can I? He didn't even bothered to try and stop me or even bothered to say no. All of my studies have concluded...that I was being used. But was Wesley used, too? Did Justin take something from him, other than his false friendship? Hey. If Wesley's psychic than why couldn't he just read Justin's mind? Unless Justin's a really good actor..., unless he knew about Wesley. How could this be? How could he have done such a thing? I feel like breaking down in tears, right here right now. They talked and watched TV while I would be having a breakdown. Why is this all happening? Isn't pregnant normally expected to be a good thing? How come *I* don't get to have a good one? How come the *father* had to ruin it?

"Al, you're being unreasonable."

'Unreasonable?' Are you serious? 'Wes, have you *seen* what he's put me through? Do you think it's fair? I don't think so!'

"Al..., please."

I see Justin's..., Justin's shadow coming from the foyer and Wes's isn't too far behind. I see Justin carrying a small plastic bag on one hand, while Wesley is carrying a cardboard box over his shoulders. I looked at them for a second and then remind myself that there are other people in the room. I look up at Bobo and Aria and then turned to look at Gloria. None of them move to help Wesley. They all just stood or sat there, looking at them. I stoop up from the couch and walked over to him, passing Justin; pretending as if he wasn't even there.

I opened my hands and was about to try and help Wesley when he looked up at me and gave me the *look*.

"What are you doing?" He said.

I managed to get at least a sense of how much it weighted before everyone else in the room stormed to stop me. Bobo was the one whose hand ran cold down my right arm. Gloria was the one who had her arms on my waist and was gently pulling me back. I could feel Ariadne's one hand one my back, it was just there.

"Step back." Wesley told everyone. "You," he looked at me. "Sit down." He said a bit exhaustedly.

"I want to help...now that no one else wants to." I turned my head a little towards them.

"Sit please." He says.

I gave up and sat in Gloria's seat with my legs crossed as I laid back and watched the scene. I tried not to look at you know who, but I could tell that he was looking at me.

Then I see Bobo and Aria both turning back around and going to the place where they used to be. Gloria just stands there. She looks back at Bobo, but he couldn't even see her because he had his back to them. Then Gloria comes and picks up the box over Wes's shoulders and holds it for a few seconds. Wesley took the box and placed it on the floor.

"...Thank you, Gloria." Wesley admired.

"...You're welcome." She blushed a little.

After that Wesley seats on the arm of the couch on my side and Gloria just stands next to the table, which is pretty close to the couch; it's behind it.

I see Justin just standing there with the plastic white bag...doing nothing. Everyone else is just minding their own business... Well, at least Bobo and Ariadne are. I waited and waited for someone to do *something*. The only thing I got was having Wesley's hand comforting my shoulder as he rubbed it.

"Hey, guys." Justin begins.

They both take their time on giving him their attention…, but they eventually do.

"…Hum…, hi."

Is he stuck? Did he gain stage fright? Should I help? 'Don't even think about it,' I told myself. Wouldn't that just be pathetic on my part?

"…So, do you guys need something?" He asked.

"…Why would you ask?" Aria asked.

"Well, you all are standing around as if there's something that somebody needs to give you. Is there?" He asked again.

"…I'm waiting for Bobo." Gloria explained.

Five seconds later and Gloria is the only one that moves. She walked over to Bobo and moved his face with her hand to kiss his cheek. As she walked over to the front door she was saying goodbye to me.

"Wait." I told her.

She walked back into the living room and stood by the living room entrance close to Justin.

"Stay, please." I begged.

She smiled down at me and nodded as she slowly sat next to me.

"Or everyone can stay." Justin disapproved.

"Is there something you're going to say?" Bobo and Wesley asked.

Justin looked at them and I did too, to see what he saw; nothing. They, like us, were waiting to see what was going on. He goes and puts down the bag and looks at me.

"Al...," he begins. "I am so sorry. I didn't get...a chance to explain myself, but I will now. I really I am sorry." He walked closer to me and kneeled. "I really, truly, am. I wish you could ever forgive me for what I'm about to tell you."

I felt like crying. Everyone huddled a bit closer to us now and they seemed to have been waiting. Gloria, being the only one, wasn't really paying attention to what he was going to say. I wanted to look back at Wes and see what he reads, but at this point my eyes are just fixed on Justin...waiting nervously on what he has to tell me. Is he going to break up with me and ask for the divorce paper? He's going to tell me that he doesn't want to be part of this family anymore, right? He's going to left as soon as I nod my head, because if he wants to go I won't stop him. Is he going to keep apologizing? Am I ever going to accept it?

"I...do love you..., and the baby..., everyone else." He tried to smile up to them all. "I did something wrong..., but I didn't know about it. I just found out a little while ago, so..., please try not to get mad." He said. He reached for my hand and took it, even though I wasn't going to give it to him. "I..." His eyes began to water. "I have Balanoaqugen."

Everyone, I could feel that everyone was staring at him...confused and disturbed at the same time, because that's how I was. I was only imagining what that was. Some kind of car he bought without my consent? Was it some kind of dog he already bought? Now, wait..., it must be some fancy new thing that he bought for baby Jack.

"What's Bala...noaqugen?" Gloria surprised me by remembering.

"..."

Justin looked up at everyone and I could see in his face that he had discovered something... Was it the fact that no one knew what it was?

"...It's a disease." He blurred out. "It's this...*thing* that comes out of a guy's...*thing* and I... *I* could give to *you*..." He stopped talking. "It's not deathly, Sweetheart." He said in a rush. "It will... It will be hard, but we can get treated."

I snapped out of myself and took back my hand from him. I almost began to cry again if it wasn't for the fact that this pisses me off. How could he have done this?

"He didn't, Al-" Wesley said.

"You stay out of it!" I yelled at him.

...What!? What's going to happen now? Will the baby be okay? Will *I* die? How long will it be until I'm...cured? Justin! Aaahahhh! The belly couldn't have stopped me from running out of that room fast enough. I ran out of the living room and into the bathroom in the kitchen. I locked myself inside and cried inside of the tub.

My whole life as been turned completely upside down in just a matter of months. I'd realize that almost everything I thought was so perfect now really isn't so perfect after all. All of these complicated scenes make me think that dealing with Seashell wasn't all that bad. Now I have a baby that I have to be good for. I have a psychic little brother and a semi-rebellious other one. I live miles..., states, away from my mother..., who I seem to be missing. I feel like I'm living a life of lies. This isn't mine..., but someone else's. It's nightmare of a life. A much unexpected nightmare of a life.

You would think that by now I've learned my lesson and learned to deal with things as unexpected as the other things that I'd dealt with..., but it's still a shock. It is still not fair. It is still not quite the life I wanted to have... This is not the kind of thing I would *ever* want to have a family under the circumstances of.

If I'd had a second chance to turn it all back, forget about everything, and to have a new life...would I take it? No. If I did I would have never learned the things I know now, or at least I wouldn't have learned them as soon. I wouldn't have gotten up to *this* point. I wouldn't be here in the tub crying about what I should do now. If I had a glimpse..., the smallest one, of what life would be like...I would never want to take a look. I would never want to ruin the unexpected surprises that would have come.

"Al." I could hear Wesley's voice as he knocked on the door.

"..."

I'm not going to open.

"Please? Let's talk. All of us..., together."
Wesley, I can't!

"Why not?"
It's too hard? How do you feel knowing that your beloved niece might end up having something wrong or different?

"...I know it's hard, Al. But if anything...you're the one that can at least try to be strong...just to make it through."
Wes. How I possibly go out there. I'm sick of all of this stress and all of these *stupid* secrets that could potentially harm *my baby* now.

"Owlina..., please. At least open the door." He said sincerely.

It took me two minutes to decide that I wanted to out of the tub. Then, it took me two other minutes to actually turn the knob to unlock the door and not just to leave my hand and on it.

I could see Wesley sitting on the floor right outside of the bathroom. Aria was sitting on the couch with her legs crossed and Gloria was leaning on the other side of the bathroom door…, on the other wall, if it makes any sense.

"Hi, Sweetie." Was Aria actually trying to sound excited?

"How are you? Are you alright?" Gloria asked.

"…Aw." Justin said.

Bobo was out in the yard, I could see him through the glass door. He was passing back and forward. What is he doing?

"He's just thinking." Wesley said as he was standing up.

I don't feel like opening my mouth…, Wesley.

"You don't have to. I'll go and make some of that soup we love so much and we can sit down and just take everything step by step. Baby steps, Al." We smiled at each other.

Wes made the soup while me and Gloria sat on the chairs by the kitchen table. Aria seemed to have been examining me with her dirty look. Justin was apparently sitting on the floor next to the couch.

"What, Ariadne?" I asked in anger.

Wesley heard me and turned his head back at me… Was he examining me, too?

"What's wrong with you?" She asks.

"Ariadne, leave it alone." Gloria said.

"…No!" She hissed at Gloria as if Gloria was an ignorant little child who didn't know anything. She was standing up now. "You're acting like if the world has just killed everyone and everything in it, it's not that bad! You haven't even heard Justin speak everything, because you're not strong enough to handle whatever he might want to say. You're just so full-"

"That's enough from you!" Wesley said pretty loudly.

"You shut up!" She told Wesley.

"No, Aria." Bobo said with his strong manly voice as he walked inside. "That is enough, and I better not hear you talk to anyone from the family like that again. You understand?" He leaned over and rested his elbows on the kitchen counter.

"...Yes."

"Good, so we are clear."

Ariadne, like a little cowardly rat, went back to sitting on her spot on the couch, or so I suppose; I couldn't see into the living room. Justin should really get up from the floor and start explaining himself before I do anything illegal.

"..." Wesley's eggs were cooking in the frying pan and the sounded delicious. "...Justin, you think that now you should explain yourself?" Wes asked him.

It took Justin a minute to stand up and walk close enough to me to see that he was crying. He sat on the chair next to me that was to my left. He looked at the table and he didn't look up to me until minutes later.

"Al...," he began. "I never meant for this to happen. I never knew or thought or even suspected that such thing would *ever* happen. I do... I truly do apologize. I am so sorry and I...can't find out how to make this up to you." He sounded... weak. "Please, I really do wish I could find out how to make you happy again."

Wesley took some plates out from a cabinet, which made some noise and gave him all of our attention. Gloria now was rubbing her hand on my hand in comfort.

"...I just found out; I wouldn't have *done anything* if I'd known." He continued. "But, Al, please forgive me. Like everything else we will and can and should get through it together. Please, just don't give up. Don't give up on us and on trying to make things better now."

"...Eat." Wesley said to me as he placed the plate of soup in front of me.

Then, he went back to go and get the other plates; all except for Ariadne's. Bobo sat next to Gloria then he and she eat out of the other's plate.

"Can we try to make this work out, Owlina?"

"What...*is* it?" I asked as I stirred my soup.

"...Well, it doesn't kill anyone or anything, so that's good. It can get passed down by...what we did. Balanoaqugen isn't really found in most people, but when it is...doctors like to make tests and try to find out things. It can be...difficult to live with; it can cause some...problems when you...pee. Apparently, not everyone has the same symptoms when it comes to Balanoaqugen. Also, like cancer, it might take some time to be detected... The good news is that if it's genetic then, it can sometimes skip a generation or two. Also, it can cause some really dangerous headaches, but Balanoaqugen isn't as terrible as other diseases. Al, it's not that-"

"Stop," I told him.

I stopped playing with my soup and took a sip from my spoon. It made me regret ever asking him what Bala- was. "Maybe sometimes things become even more difficult than what they used to be to *make* you learn something from it?" These words I heard from that old lady that had gotten jumped so many years ago. She told us how her daughter died...of cancer and that her being jumped wasn't any less painful. She learned how not to hold grudged over people that day that her daughter had died. Have I learned something from all of this…and from that lady and from my entire experience? Will I ever?

I drank/ate my soup and kept Justin waiting. He was eating his too, but he wanted to know why I had stopped hm. Gloria had finished hers all time ago, along with Wesley and Bobo. Now that I think about it, Ariadne wasn't even at the couch. I only saw…the couch when I went to go and put the plate in the sink.

"Leave it there, Al." Wesley told me.

Apparently, he was sitting next to Justin. Justin had finished his in just a matter of minutes while I had been taking a few seconds. Was the sudden shock of being a victim of Bala made me gain super fast speed to finish soup? After everyone had finished their soup, Wesley's kindhearted self decided to clean up the mess and told everyone to move to the living room to continue or talking. Now, it was me, Wesley was back on the couch's arm, Gloria was next to me, and Bobo was next to her. Justin had pulled up a chair from the living room table and placed it in front of me.

"Do you want to go home?" Bobo asked Gloria, his arm was around her and they looked close to adorable.

"No, I want to stay." She answered him with a simple tap of her hand to his chest. Like Rose had done to her fiancé on Titanic.

"…" Justin seemed like if he didn't want to continue.

"Are you finished?" Wesley asked him.

Justin couldn't answer because at that time the phone was ringing. Bobo was closest to the phone so he was the one to answer it. It took a while for the other person on the phone to answer his hello.

"Yes. Who's this?" Bobo asked.

He stayed quiet for about a minute and then handed me the phone. I stood up from the couch and walked over to it. When I got it Bobo went back to his seat and I stood there listening and waiting.

"Owlina?" A familiar voice called out softly from the other line.

"Yes." I said unsurely.

"...I'm so glad to hear from you. I miss talking to you and I miss our conversations and I miss hanging out with you **period**. I really wanted to talk to you but I didn't have this number, so when I called the other one...*John* gave me this one and told me to never say anything to you, but I couldn't hold that secret."

"...Kirsten?" I asked.

"Yes! Did you just wake up? Did I bother you? Should I hang up? Wait no, I can't! I really have to tell you something, Owl Cracker."

It took me a while to realize that Kirsten was on the phone. She'd called John and asked him to give her my new number because she has to tell me something. How important could this be?

"You remember how I told you that Penelope and I got married? Well, not long after the whole wedding and everything, she decided to tell me that she had a kid. Owlina, I need you to listen very carefully to me. This kid is your husband's son."

There is just no way that this could happen..., because she had an abortion. **RIGHT**? I can't be some strange brat's stepmother. I can't have my husband's son being...not *my* son. He's a father?

"Owl?" She asked. "Penelope told me that she never meant to have *not* aborted the kid, but she wanted him. She didn't care if Justin was in the picture or not, she just wanted to just birth to her little boy. Al, Penny is sorry. I would have told you sooner if I would've known... Are you okay?"

There was no sound coming from my side of the line. I could answer her, I wouldn't answer her. Penelope's thought-to-be-death son is suddenly coming back to being a very important subject. I won't answer Kirsten if I'm okay, because I'm not. I won't pretend that I'm okay, because I'm not. I can't do anything, but try to go through out this pregnancy without killing myself and Justin's **other** kid. The next thing I know is that Wesley is taking the phone away from me and making me sit on one of the chairs from the kitchen table.

"Yes..., yes..., yes. Hi! Yes... Shut up, Kirsten!" Wesley told her. "This isn't the time for you to be saying such things. Owlina is very delicate right now and it's *completely* rude of you to *even think* about *telling* her such a thing."

He was quiet for some time and then he said yes. Did he tell her that I am pregnant? Either way, he talked a bit more with her and after a short moment he gave me the phone back. As I took it I could see that he was going to go and get some water out of the fridge.

"Owlina." Kirsten said.
"Yeah?" I asked.
"...I hope you forgive me...I didn't know you were... pregnant. I wouldn't have if I have known. It...must be so awkward."

'Awkward? Completely the opposite.'
"I want you to talk or just listen...okay?" That's all she told me before she left the phone.

When I heard static I turned my attention to Wesley, he was coming over to me with a glass of cold water. He left it right in front of me and went somewhere behind me, I couldn't see.

"...Hello?" A person said.

"..." I hummed.

"...I'm Penny. Is this Owlina?"

Her voice was warm and calm, but nervous..., and yet still and gentle and tender and welcoming.

"... Uh huh." I couldn't believe it.

"Hi. We have a lot to talk about. Uh, Kirsten just told me that you're pregnant. Is that true?" She asked.

"... Uh, yes."

"I know it's difficult to even try to understand, but I did have Justin's son. I know I should be taking it easy on you, but I don't exactly have all of the time in the world. Owlina, I lied about ever having an abortion because at the time Aria and Justin were all moving from me, because of me. I didn't wanted this to be any more intricate for him back then, that's way I lied. I told him that he didn't have to worry about anything and that was that. Now, Jared keeps asking more and more questions about his father and I don't think I can keep hiding them from each other for much longer. Do you understand?"

I understand. She's a mother. Maybe when my kid comes out I would think the same way she did, but I'm not her.

"Yes."

"Thank goodness. Did you think...? Would you mind if they meet?"

"...My husband meeting his son, no I don't mind."

I meant to say this in my mind, but I had realized I didn't when she thanked me.

"Well, Owlina. I really am thankful. When Jared gets older and I explain everything to him, I will make sure that he thanks you. If you want I can let you talk to Kirsten, but I have to go and pick Jared up from soccer practice. He was so happy when he got the news that he was going to be goalie. I'm so proud of-"

"No, I'm fine. I have things to take care of here."

She thanked me one last time before hanging up. I took the glass of water and griped my fingers around it. Was I trying to pretend that the glass was Penny? Was I   trying to choke her? Either way, I loosen my grip and drank as much water as I could in less than thirty seconds. I drank it all. Had I just spoke to Penny? To the woman who I blame for my latest problems? I decided that later I would call her, thanks to caller id. I will find out if Penny was the one that gave Justin Balanoaqugen? She gave this to me and to my baby. How could I have possibly agreed to Justin meeting his kid? But if Penny gave it to Justin...does this mean that her kid has it, too? Balanoaqugen is really starting to be a pest. I decided that I must go back and listening to Justin explain and talk and murmur about it to see what I'm up against.

"Who was that?" Justin asked me.

"...Keep going." I told him.

"...I told you everything I know. Headaches, difficulties peeing, there's not much I know. Remember, I just found out, but I still don't think we should worry about it affecting the baby's growth."

He was coming in to rub my belly when I leaned back in the couch, trying to make sure that he didn't touch either of us. Had I gotten that phone call earlier would I have even *thought* about trying to convince Justin's kid? I don't think so. Now that I know that a Jared Van Berg exists somewhere in Nier...would I dare tell the father now? Probably not. I feel dizzy; I don't think I can be put through so much pressure.

And what gives with my pregnancy? I'm like two months pregnant... How come I'm growing bit by bit? I'm starting to think that this baby will be fat.

Wesley decided that it was best for everyone to just sleep off all of the drama and that tomorrow we *might* be able to continue. I was awakened by the sun's light that crept from the curtains in the room. I was alone in the bed all scattered around. I stood up and my head was rushing faster than what I had time to even think. There was an aspirin on the nightstand next to a cup of water. I took it. Probably Wesley knew that this would happen. I went to the bathroom, brushed my teeth, took a bath and got dressed. I went downstairs and I didn't feel any fatter than before. So I think that's good.

As I took my time going to the kitchen I'd realize that Jared had to be dead. Why wouldn't Penny tell Ariadne when Ariadne is like her sister? Why is it that Jared is even asking questions about his father *now*? I just don't understand what's real or not anymore.

"Let it go, Al." Said a much too in-a-hurry Wesley.

"Where are you going?" I asked as I made my way to the last few steps.

"...To the hospital, Daisy said I could go now."

I walked over to the couch and sat there, looking at him as he ran back and forth in a hurry.

"...When you come back...can we go to Phlox?" I asked him.

He stopped in the middle the foyer and the living room and turned back to look at me, I could see that he wanted to smile, but he didn't.

"Sure." He walked up to me and kissed my forehead. "I'll see you later."

He then ran out of the living room and in the kitchen. I could hear the sound of keys being rattled around, and then he dashed out into the living room, and into the foyer and out of the door.

I just stayed there on the couch for a bit. Looking around, listening to the very welcomed silence. I wondered where everyone was. I could go to the kitchen and see if anyone's there, but I stayed in my little silent moment. Then I leaned back and pulled up my shirt. I could see my little baby bump pretty well. As I rubbed it gently I felt better. Does he like it when I rub him? I wouldn't know since I never really do rub him. Then...out of nowhere, he kicked. I was happy, excited, scared, curious, terrified, *I felt motherly*. The only conclusion that came to mind was that I wasn't two months pregnant. I must have just thought that I was when I really wasn't. I wondered if when he's out and we have conversations...would he judge me for thinking wrong, for not being sure of how many months I was? Or was it possible for a two-month-old baby to kick already? I wouldn't know. I haven't gone to the library and there's still no important information on TV about dealing with husbands and their ex-lovers and their thought-to-be-dead sons.

I'm pregnant. This makes me happy. I don't know how things will differ in a couple of months, but I know that Wes will be with me, to help me out. I will have the baby. He will grow up well, not like I did, but at least as sane as I did.

I heard a loud sound that came from the kitchen. It sounded like a plate that had just been broken. I walked over and realized that Ariadne was the in front of a pile of broken little bits of a plate while Justin was sitting on one of the chairs from the table.

"... Oh. Hi, Al." Ariadne sounded as though she had been crying.

She was, because she cleaned her eyes as she walked over to hug me.

"What's going on?" I asked when I had the chance to breathe.

"Oh, nothing, I was about to slip and had the plate in my hand. I'm sorry. I'll get this cleaned up and I will pay for it. Silly little me. I can make you some scrambled eggs and some bacon if you'd like." She said.

Over the years I've realized two things; one is that I still can't believe that I am friends with such a kind of person. And two is that I know when she's lying, but she is really good and she was clearly lying now.

"That's not true, Ariadne. What's going on?" I asked Justin.

"...I might leave." He told me without looking at me, but looking at his hands on the table.

"What!?"

I almost passed out, but I'd remembered what my little monster had done not long ago. This brought me back to full consciousness in no time.

Ariadne helped me to a chair...away from him.

"Explain. Now!" I said as I was trying to catch my breath.

"...Wesley told me what happened yesterday...on the phone. Al, if I have a kid out there and he wants to meet me than I can't say no. Can I? No, I can't. I'm thinking about going down to Nier to see...Jared."

"...I'm not simply a few months pregnant." I confessed.

They both looked at me as if I was truly going crazy. I would have thought so too if it wasn't for this little guy kicking just now.

"Yes, you are. You said so." Justin said.

"No, I'm not. How many two-month-old babies do you know that can kick?" I asked.

"He kicked?" Ariadne rushed to my side and was going to rub my belly.

"What? Al, that's insane. Are you making this up?" Justin said, then Ariadne leaned back and stood up straight.

"Al, are you?" She asked.

"...No." I answered. "He just kicked but stopped when Ariadne scared me with the plate."

"...I'm sorry." She said.

"...It was wonderful. I was scared, but he made me feel safe in some way. It was magnificent."

"...I'm going to Nier to see Jared. I don't know if there's going to be some arrangement for me to go see him every week or something, but I'll talk to Penny about that." He went back to that subject.

"...I think I'll have some of our amazing eggs, Ariadne."

"Alright, Sweetie," She rubbed my back and went into the fridge.

I was watching nothing but oblivion now; waiting for some miracle to happen. Ariadne was taking forever to make some stupid eggs and Justin, just being there, wasn't making things any easier for me. Now I'm thinking..., does he even want me anymore? Why does he care about this more than me? **I'M THE ONE THAT'S PREGANT HERE!** The hell! He doesn't need to go out to Nier to see some brat that was meant to be DEAD! It's all Penny's fault! If she hadn't ever lied then maybe, I wouldn't be in this situation.

"I don't want his to go! How dare he just think that he can get up and leave me...again!? I can't stand this! I need to leave. I need to go out and see dad, see how mom's doing. I doubt that any of this bullshit is good for me! I can't believe I have to choose between having him here or having him with his meant-to-be-dead kid. The fuck!?"

I wasn't meant to say *any* of this out loud. Why can't I learn how to shut my mouth better rather than how to become angrier and angrier?

"Al!" Justin's shocked voice called out.

I shook my head in disbelief and disapproval. I walked over to get my keys from the hook on the wall and I made my way to the driveway. I was ready to just take my car and runaway completely, but the thought that I was pregnant held me back. I got in my car and turned up the radio as loud as possible. It comforts me the way my husband wouldn't dare to now.

I wanted to cry, but wouldn't that just make me look weaker? Since when do I care about looking weak? I cried. Holding on to the steering wheel, listening to Teenagers by My Chemical Romance, crying my guts out, I was being healed. The music was healing me in a way that could be mistaken as magically. I was feeling amazing all thanks to...me crying? No. I thank My Chemical Romance for always being there for me, even when they don't know it. Thank you. Thank you to so many more. Green Day, Linkin Park, Avril, Pink, Escape the Fate, Bring Me the Horizon, the Misfits, Boys like Girls, you all and too many more have been there for me. How could I ever thank you? Should I go buy your albums? Should I make a shrine? All I know is that I have to go and leave and not come back to Wichita for a long while. I need to be with my father. I need to be with my baby. I need to be with my music.

I put the keys in the ignition and turned it. My baby purred with pride. It wasn't long until I was on the road. No sign of Justin on my tail, no sign of Wesley, nothing. I'd realized that I'm by myself and I liked it. Having to *not* listen to some bitchy complaint all the time; I'm having fun. I drove up to the station to fill up my tank. Inside at the cash register a young kid assisted me.

"Hello there, might I be of service to you, ma'am?" She asked.

"I just came to fill in my tank." I pointed to my car. "Is that okay with you?"

"Well of course." She was your typical girl from Texas or Tennessee, that western ascent doesn't come much from here.

Minutes later I was driving out of the station and into the highway. Where was I planning on going? I don't know. I let my car take me where ever he felt like we should go. He wanted to go back to Phlox, I know the way, way too well.

Moments after moments after moments after moments later, I get to the cemetery. The first thing that comes to mind is...'where's Justin watering the trees?' Then I though...'oh.' So, I turned off the car and looked at the gates with love. As I make my way out of the car and shut the door I think that I am back home..., back with Seashell. I've missed her? Yes. I've missed my mother. I opened the gates, they screeched like always. I laughed, because it seemed like forever ago that I was here and that I was here for good reasons. I don't even know exactly why I had come this far for. What was my reason exactly? I took my time. I passed the secondary most favorite tree of mine as I walked by. I passed The Store and I could see The Garage not far from it. The displays in The Store's windows tell me that Lara wasn't the manager anymore; she would never place such a thing there for everyone to look at. I walked into it. There was a woman there with orange hair stacking boxes on shelves.

"Uh, hello. Sorry. Can I help you?" She asked when I rang the little silver bell on the counter..., which was my idea.

"...One Irish please."

She shook her head and left me. When she returned she had a gorgeous purple Irish in her hand. I paid her, she thanked me, and I was free to go see my father. It took me some time to get there, because I wanted to go visit my tree. My...Willow. My Willow tree, my mother of all mother-roots... had been chopped down. The stump was there...; it looked lonely. I fell on my knees and I cried. Why would anyone ever even think of doing such a thing? I was heartbroken. My heart was mending and now it had been officially ripped apart. It was ripped right out of me, completely throbbing to me, it was burned and they threw away the ashes in some garbage can. My whole life revolved around Wesley and the car...and this tree. Why?

I can't even make proper sentences without having to think about how horrifying this is..., without thinking that my life is truly over. For some time, for the time I've been back, I haven't thought of where my things are at... At that place that I've believed was truly my home, but now I know better than to even want to return to that place. Well, I know that I will *have* to go back sooner or later..., I just don't want to. I don't want to have to deal with Justin and Ariadne and Penny and that damn it Jared. A few minutes later, I wasn't up yet. I was still crying. A man's voice cried out to me, wondering if I was okay. I told him everything. I sat on the ground and told him everything. He sat next to me and we talked. He made *me* feel as though it wasn't my fault, but it was just inevitable. That none of it had been my fault and that even if I could change anything, it would have highly happen *again*. I felt better, though. This kind and handsome stranger must be from here. Phlox has a lot of kindhearted people, excluding my mother and John. He gave me his number and told me that if I or my brothers or my baby needed his help that he's just seven digits away, or ten.

After we had finished our conversation, it was dad's turn. I told him everything I told Gerard and more. Gerard, the stranger, was kind, but there is just no comparison when it comes to my father. He was bright and present and alert, like he used to be. Some tears came out, and when enough didn't come out I figured that I had run out of tears for the day. Daddy was amazing. He always was that one person I could go to, that one really good and brave guy. He made me his little princess again. I just feel ecstatic to be here and yet horrible about my tree. That was the place I wanted to spend all eternity in. My talk with dad was longer than any other one I had *ever* truly had. The Irish went where it always went to and my love for my father as well.

I stopped my car in front of Seashell's house. I didn't want to go in and I wasn't exactly planning on it either. I could see the living room from the window; they had opened the curtains pretty wide. After about a minute, I saw them. They were dancing back and forth in the room. I smiled. Mom looked normal as she danced with John. They looked happy, like if they were really normal and having fun. This made me think..., there are so many people out there that look like this, normal. They look like they really do love each other, when on the inside there's so much bullshit going on it's almost impossible to explain. I left not long after that. I was heading back to Wichita. I didn't wanted to, I didn't have to. I looked for a phone booth instead. It seemed insane really, but I called Gerard. He told me I could stay with him for the night if I really felt like there wasn't another choice, he didn't mind. The most unexpected thing was that Gerard lived on Justin's old street. The same street that you have to pass heaven to get to, that's where Gerard lives. Gerard could have been Justin's seventh neighbor down.

How crazy have I become? I parked my love in his driveway and knocked the door several times before he opened it. He had an apron on and I wanted to laugh. His hair floated down his ears like a beautiful waterfall. He told to come in and I did. The rest of the time was amazing. Apparently, he was cooking for me and it was delicious... It was baked Rigatoni topped with melted provolone cheese *and* Linguini with White Clam Sauce, homemade clam sauce. He told me that his Italian mother passed away not long ago, leaving tons of recipes that could *literately* last a lifetime. We played board games and chatted. We watched this movie... The Notebook. It made me cried. After that movie I'd realized that Nicolas Sparks was my favorite author. In the morning, I woke up to the smell of eggs. I've had too many eggs in my mind.

"Good morning." He welcomed me as I walked into the kitchen.

"Hi."

"..." He looked at me. "You don't like eggs?"

"...I do, but my...sister-in-law made took forever to make some the other day... I'm not really up for eggs."

"Oh, no problem. There's still a bit of pasta left from last night if you'd like. Or I can make something else." He turned around and cleaned his hands in the sink.

He went to look for something in a cabinet, and then he turned and showed me his mother's book of lifetime recipes. We laughed together and had fun. I threw up at the very sight of the eggs in the pot. The kindhearted man told me that there was a toothbrush he didn't use in the bathroom and that I should go get cleaned up while he cleaned up the floor.

A week past and I was still in Gerard's house. I told him that I had to go back..., back to Wichita. I had a life there. I left his house one day with new clothes that he'd bought me and I took off. The road seemed much nicer that what it did eight days ago.

It wasn't long until I got there. Justin nor Ariadne nor Wesley nor Bobo were home. It seemed as though it was just me again. As I went up to my room I was thinking of getting my suitcases and packing them, leaving everyone and everything behind. Then, I heard the phone ringing downstairs. I peeked my head out of the room to see if anyone was going to get it. Then I heard...

"Hello?" Was that Bobo? "Not that I would know. It's not my fault, Wes! Well, excuse me, but I'm the one not to blame!" He was quiet for a while. When he began to talk I couldn't hear; he was too soft for my ears. "In my room." He was quiet again. "Okay, okay. Bye." I heard the click and then I went back to packing, quietly, with the door as closed as possible.

It was harder now to pack. I was planning on just packing and leaving the Wichita Mountains forever. I had no idea what I was going to leave Wesley and Bobo. But, they *are* adults now and they can take care of themselves. Maybe it's just time for us to end up taking a different road instead of taking that same one together. I sat on the bed, wondering and thinking. How could I do this? About sixteen years ago I wouldn't have ever even thought about this. I wouldn't have ever even wanted to leave their side. Did Gerard change all of that? Or was it just faith? Was it the way that things ended up between Justin and me? Either way it was, I was now determined to leave this place and turned my life around. Raise my kid somewhere else with someone I've fallen in love with. I never meant to fall in love with anyone else but the baby's father. It's funny how things can be unexpected like that.

"Al?"

The door opened a bit as I saw a ball of curly blonde hair coming through. Bobo's face popped out and shocked me. It's only been a week, right? He didn't look the same. I really couldn't see what was different, but he didn't look the same. He came into the room completely now and I could see that he wasn't even dressed the same. He looked proper, really proper. As if, he wasn't even my Bobo anymore but some duplicate of him with different clothes. His face up and then I realized what was different. He's gorgeous, childlike face was not happy. I blamed myself. He ran to me then.   I responded immediately to his rush and stood up. We fit into that hug perfectly. I could hear his sniffing as he began to cry. I then realize what I had done. I couldn't believe what I have done.

"Don't cry." I tried to comfort him.

He didn't stop. He didn't stop crying at all. It was like I had no voice anymore and he couldn't hear me, but he *could* feel me. I felt terrible, never in my life have I seen him crying over something that I have done. Why did I do that? How can I leave now?

It wasn't long until he finally stopped crying and we stopped hugging. I could see his eyes were red from crying. I wiped his tears away as I apologized. He didn't answer.

"Bobo, please, I'm so sorry."

"...If you were really sorry then you wouldn't have done it."

His voice was deeper, like a country artist. I miss his voice. Didn't I say that before, once? Now that I have heard and hurt him, I'm left to wonder what I must do now.

"You left, Al. You swore that you'd *never* leave us, *ever*! You broke your promise!" He yelled.

At this point two things were running though my head; one is what have I gotten myself into. And two was what have I done. I doubt now that I could ever go back to Gerard even if they let me go.

'But, what about Wesley?'

Would Wesley treat me like a monster now that I've... returned? How could I even think of anything like that? I am now more regretful than I ever have. Or am I? Am I really sorry? I mean I did have fun with Gerard, and how could my family keep me away from the person I've fallen in love with? If I explain myself really well..., would they let me go? Or would they even want to come with me? *Would* Wesley and Bobo ever even want to come with me back to Phlox and live me with and Gerard? What's left to do now? I hadn't planned for this to happen. It was just suppose to be me and packing and me with my bags back to Gerard forever.

"Al, are you leaving us? Are you leaving for good?" He asked.

His gaze was locked on my bags and mine was locked on his terrified, and destroyed, and devastated, and suffering face. I thought only about me and what I wanted now.

"I am leaving." I told him.

He lift up his face and looked and me. "NO, you can't!"

"Actually, I can, Bobo. I'm done staying somewhere that I don't want to. I went to Phlox and I met a guy. I've fallen in love."

"It was only eight days." He said in a way that showed that he didn't believe me.

"It was long enough for me to realize what I had been missing out. Me and the baby are going to Gerard's house and we're going to stay there. You and Wesley will always be welcomed to come along, but I *am* leaving and no one can stop me anymore."

It was as if something had possessed me and that caused me to do this. It had caused me my happiness with my baby brother. Will he ever forgive me now? All I was doing was trying to be happy. How come it's a crime? I don't want to explain myself and I don't want anyone to judge me for it. Is that too much to ask from the ones who I've taken care of since forever?

"You can't leave! I still need you, Al!" He yelled as I went back to packing.

A second later I heard a, "Let her go, Bobo. We'll let her go."

I turned my head and saw my darling brother standing there at the door. I ran and hugged him, and he welcomed me with open arms. I felt like I was back home, but in theory I wasn't. I was just happy that I was with my brother..., brothers.

"So you are leaving." He told me when we released each other.

"...I am. I want to. You two can come with." I offered.

"I'm making a live here with Brook. I can't leave her, Al." Wesley answered.

"I'm with Gloria here." Bobo was calming down now.

"So what? Is this were we separate?" I asked.

"Wasn't it coming sooner or later?" Wesley joked.

"NO!" Bobo disagreed.

"Come here, boys."

I opened my arms and they both, taller than me, bigger than me, hugged me. It was a happy and a sad moment. I hadn't planned it, but it *just happened*. It was unexpected like that, like everything else. I finished hugging them and finished telling them that everything will be just fine and that this isn't the end.

"Can we at least come visit you?" Bobo asked me.

"Are you kidding? Of course, Gerard has guest rooms if you wish to stay over or anything." I responded.

The boys helped me get my things into my car, all of my things. I left the address and the number of my new home. We hugged each other goodbye. That was that. Thanks to Wesley I left with a clean slate. I wondered if Justin was going to me mad. I wondered if Ariadne was going to me mad at me. I wondered a lot of things. Like if I was left with having to give birth to the baby with Gerard as his new father.

Months later and I became a mother. Something much unexpected happened, I was carrying twins. Baby Rebecca Kayla Wellheart and baby Tyson Devin Wellheart were born on October 19th of this hectic 2026 year. Apparently, I *am* a great mother and so is Gerard. He is always making jokes when we're changing the kids. Justin came once to see them, at the hospital. I don't know much about him and Penny and Jared. I talk to Aria once or twice a month on the phone and she's very supportive, though not as supportive as Gloria. Wesley and Bobo, so darling, love the twins and the twins can't get enough of them. Brook is actually planning on having a baby, so then maybe the twins won't grow up alone after all. Bobo says that he doesn't want any children, but Gloria can be demanding, like her mother, who I got the pressure to meet one night over dinner here. Gloria and Bobo couldn't be anymore adorable than Wesley and Brook. Now, things are good and I just wondered if everything is *officially* going to stay this way. I don't pray, but I pray that everything will be fine. Everything will as long as my daddy's and my 1967 Chevy Impala takes me to my happiness.